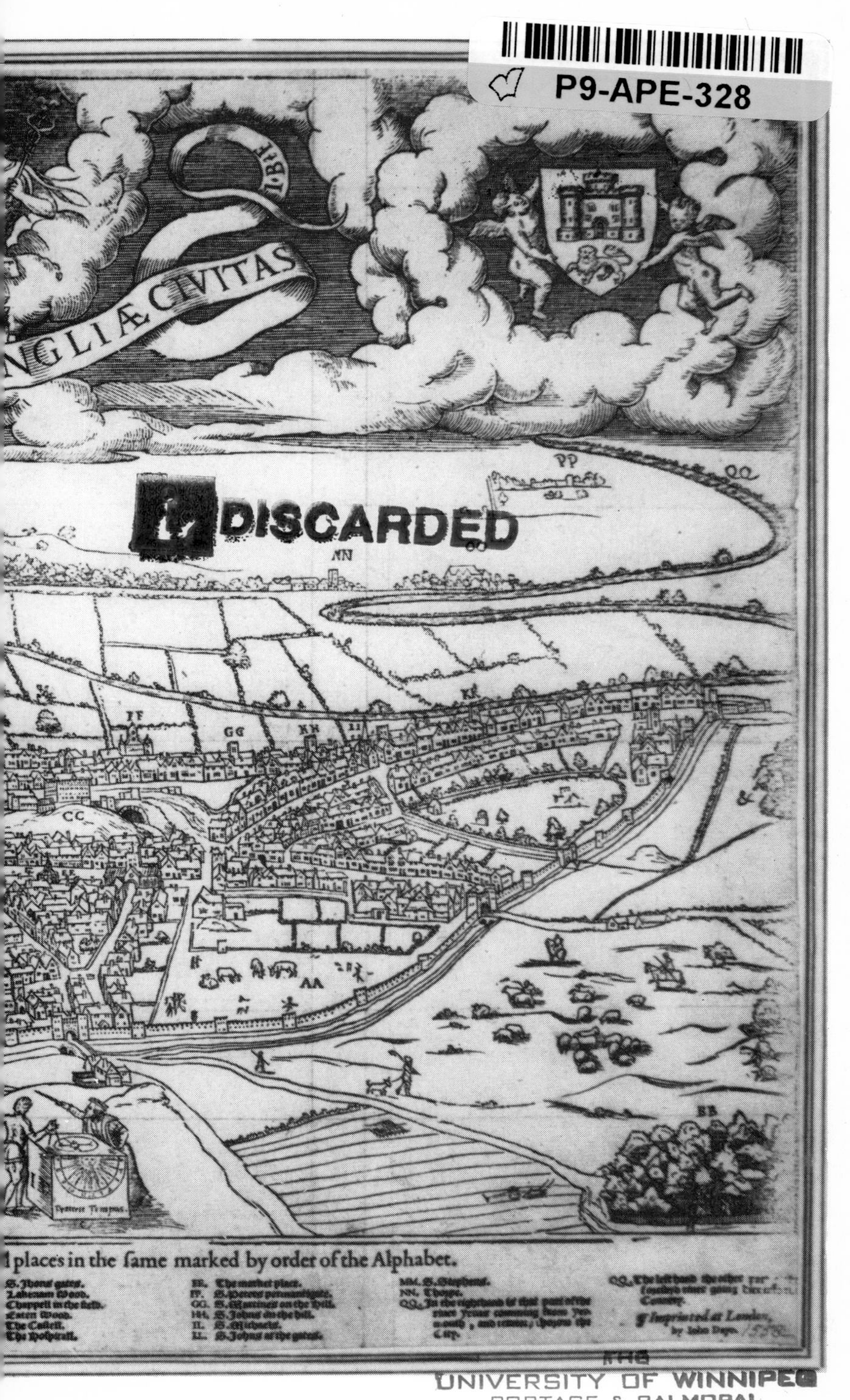
NGLIÆCIVITAS
PP
QQ
NN
FF
GG
HH
CC
AA
BB
places in the same marked by order of the Alphabet.
Imprinted at London,
by John Daye.

KETT'S REBELLION

The Norfolk Rising of 1549

Lord Protector Somerset

(Photo Courtauld Institute, reproduced by permission of the Marquess of Bath, Longleat House)

KETT'S REBELLION

The Norfolk Rising of 1549

STEPHEN K. LAND

THE BOYDELL PRESS · ROWMAN & LITTLEFIELD

Published by The Boydell Press Ltd
PO Box 24 Ipswich IP1 1JJ

First published 1977

First published in the USA 1977 by
Rowman and Littlefield 81 Adams Drive
Totowa NJ 07512

Cataloguing in Publication Data
Land, Stephen K.
Kett's rebellion.
1. Kett's Rebellion, 1549
I. Title
942.05'3 DA 345

ISBN 0-85115-084-5
US ISBN 0-87471-995-X

Printed and bound in Great Britain by
Redwood Burn Limited
Trowbridge & Esher

Contents

Preface

The outline of Kett's rebellion of 1549 can be found in any account of the reign of Edward VI, but reliable narratives of the details of the rising are few and difficult to find outside the larger libraries. Sixteenth-century accounts of the rebellion all derive from two sources, of which only one is a direct eye-witness narration. Since then only two studies, those of Blomefield and Russell, have contributed significantly to our knowledge of the course of events. Recent historical scholarship, however, has thrown much light on the social and economic causes of the rising. The present work combines a retelling of the events of Kett's rebellion with a summary of what twentieth-century scholars have discovered concerning its background and origins.

Besides recounting the story I have tried to place the Norfolk rising in the context of national politics, and for this reason I begin with the death of Henry VIII in 1547 and include the fall of Somerset in 1549. The Norfolk rising was, in a peculiar way, a product of the policies of Protector Somerset and was one of the factors contributing to his overthrow. It was, nonetheless, primarily a local affair, and I have tried to show how conditions in Norfolk in 1549 first allowed the rising to achieve some success but later prevented its growth and thus ensured its eventual suppression. The several genealogies given in the text are directed to this point, for Kett was opposed not simply by local lawyers and landowners but by a network of familial ties among the gentry, which included some of the foremost English soldiers and statesmen of the day.

The traditional view of the events of the rebellion sees Kett as the strong, silent champion of the oppressed commons and Somerset as the "good Duke", the humanist nobleman, overthrown by Warwick, the unscrupulous, plotting warrior-lord. There is, of course, a grain of truth in this, but it is much too simple. The known facts suggest that Warwick generally acted with humanity and integrity, that Somerset's policy of meeting economic problems with enclosure commissions was responsible for much of the unrest of 1549, and that Kett's followers were not, by sixteenth-century standards, particularly oppressed.

The only eye-witness account of the events of the Norfolk rising is Nicholas Sotherton's *The Commoyson in Norfolk 1549*. Son of a Mayor of Norwich and himself a city alderman, Sotherton is understandably unsympathetic towards the rebels. An important supplementary source is Alexander Neville's *De furoribus Norfolciensium Ketto duce* published in 1575 and translated into English in 1615 by Richard Woods under the title *Norfolke Furies.* Neville's account was appended under the title *Kettus* to Christopher Ocland's *Anglorum Praelia* in 1582. Neville was prompted to undertake the work by Archbishop Parker who had connections in Norfolk and who had been present for some days in Norwich during the rising. Although he wrote twenty-five years after the events and had himself no first-hand knowledge, Neville's account is of particular value because it certainly incorporates Parker's reminiscences.

The recently published journals of Edward VI include a brief outline of the rising which is of interest as a contemporary document by one who had access to the best information. Two other early accounts, those given in Holinshed's *Chronicles* (1578) and Hayward's *Life and Reign of King Edward the Sixth* (1610), have little to add.

The two essential printed narratives by later historians are those of Blomefield and Russell. Francis Blomefield (1705–1752) began publishing his great history of Norfolk in 1739 but died whilst working on the third volume. The work was finished by others, particularly by Charles Parkin, and the first edition was completed in 1775. (I have used the second edition because it is easier to find and is more often referred to by modern historians.) The account of the rising is given in the history of the city of Norwich which was completed by Blomefield himself. A member of an old Norfolk family and by profession a clergyman, Blomefield was a Tory and disinclined to favour popular uprisings, but his narrative is detailed and accurate. Frederick W. Russell, in *Kett's Rebellion in Norfolk* (1859), also gives a reliable narrative and reprints in a series of appendices a most valuable collection of documents and other materials relating to the rising.

More recent tellings of the tale have been less useful. Joseph Clayton (1912) is somewhat rhetorical and often misleading, although his open sympathy for the rebel cause came as a needed corrective to the strictures of Sotherton and Blomefield. Groves' book, published in 1947 by the Red Flag Fellowship, has a similar orientation. Neither of these makes any serious attempt to explain Kett's rebellion in terms of its historical context.

Twentieth-century scholarship has unearthed little to add to the narrative but has done much to elucidate the events of the rising by studying its context – the political, social, and economic condition of England in the reign of Edward VI. Of the first importance are the studies of A. F. Pollard (1900 and 1913) and R. H. Tawney (1912), although these must be supplemented, in the fields of political and economic history respectively, by Bush (1975) and Kerridge (1969). An invaluable application of new perspectives to an explanation of the rising is S. T. Bindoff's *Ket's Rebellion,* a pamphlet published by the Historical Association in 1949. Brief summaries of current historical interpretation of the Norfolk rebellion can be found in Fletcher (1968) and Foss (1973).

Of the many general surveys of the period of the Protectorate I have relied particularly upon Jordan (1968) and Bush (1975) for my account of political events. The *Dictionary of National Biography* has yielded information on many of the minor characters of the story. My references to buildings and places in Norfolk are frequently indebted to LeStrange (1973) and Pevsner (1962). In addition I have drawn on a number of studies of particular persons, places, and events. Specific references are given in the footnotes: a bibliographical list of all works cited follows the text. I have not, however, given footnote references to factual material drawn from the four "classical" sources (Sotherton, Neville, Blomefield, and Russell) except where a particular passage is quoted or cited or where the matter involved is one of opinion.

The reliance of the present study upon the writings just mentioned will be obvious. On a more personal level I am indebted to my late grandfather – himself born within a mile or two of Wymondham – who first encouraged me to think about Norfolk, and to my father whose generosity has done much to make my work possible.

Stephen K. Land

1. *The Lord Protector*

In the early hours of the morning of Friday, 28 January, 1547, Henry VIII died in the royal palace at Westminster. His health had been declining for some time, but almost until the last Henry refused to tolerate mention of approaching death. Only on the evening of the day before had his attendant Sir Anthony Denny, Chief Gentleman of the Bedchamber and a trusted friend, ventured to suggest that a priest should be summoned. Accordingly Archbishop Cranmer was called from Croydon to minister to the speechless and dying King. Henry died aged fifty-five in the thirty-eighth year of his reign. Nineteen days later he was buried in St. George's Chapel at Windsor in the tomb which already held the remains of Queen Jane Seymour, his third wife, whom it seems he had truly loved and who had died after the birth of his only son. Edward VI, the single surviving male child of Henry's six marriages, was a minor of only nine years when by his father's death he became King of England.

Henry's desire to secure the succession of the crown to the house of Tudor had been the most consistent and far-reaching motive of his policy. To divorce his first wife, Catherine of Aragon, who bore him no sons, he risked the enmity of her Habsburg relations, rulers of Spain and the Holy Roman Empire, and at the same time severed the English church from Rome because Pope Clement VII, under pressure from the Habsburgs, refused to nullify the marriage. To ensure the succession of his children by subsequent unions Henry completed the breach with Rome by the Act of Supremacy, which established him as head of the English church. He proceeded to dissolve the monasteries, using a great deal of the lands and monies which they yielded to create and aggrandize a new nobility whose loyalties and interests would ally them to the Tudor dynasty. In addition Henry, who had been empowered by Parliament to nominate his successor, left a will.

The will provided for a government during the minority of Edward VI of sixteen councillors, all of whom were either members of the newly-created nobility or statesmen who owed their promotion to Henry. The Council was to govern as a body, and not to be dominated by any single man or party. As the King, in theory, governs in the interest of the realm and not of any faction, so the Council was to govern during the minority not for their own ends but for the good of the kingdom. Accordingly, although the Council contained a high proportion of Protestants and reformers, Henry also included several conservative pro-Catholics, such as Lord Chancellor Wriothesley and Bishop Tunstall of Durham, as well as two judges, and several experienced statesmen, like Sir William Paget, who were not strongly committed to either the Catholics or the reformers. Yet this Council was in the event dominated in succession by two of its original members, Edward Seymour, Earl of Hertford, shortly to be created Duke of Somerset, and John Dudley, Viscount Lisle, shortly to become Earl of Warwick and later Duke of Northumberland. Even as Henry lay dying Hertford and Paget conferred in the galleries of Westminster outside the King's chamber and determined that the will, which seems to have been in Hertford's keeping, should not be strictly executed. They decided that the news of the King's death should be kept secret in order to allow them time to override the will's requirement that the Council govern as a body and to secure the nomination of Hertford as Lord Protector of the realm.

Henry's death and the accession of the boy king Edward left a vacuum at the centre of power. Since the defeat of Richard III at Bosworth in 1485 England had experienced a period of internal stability as a result of the strong and largely personal governments of Henry VII and Henry VIII. For over sixty years the administration had depended continuously and heavily upon the will of the king, but for the ten or so years of Edward's minority there would be no effective royal authority. Men thought back to the similar situation which had arisen over one hundred years before when the succession of the child Henry VI to the power and empire acquired by his father and grandfather led to a prolonged period of civil war among powerful barons. Henry's bequest of the regency to a Council of sixteen named executors was designed to prevent degeneration of the central authority into factional conflict by a balanced representation of the Council of the major interests in the country.

The scheme was surely foredoomed. Even had such a balance of forces been achieved the Council could hardly have continued to govern as a single body for very long, and it could not have perpetuated its equilibrium through the ten or so years of Edward's minority. The only realistic alternative to the eventual dissolution of the regency government into a struggle among warring factions was the choice of one strong man who could be expected to rule moderately and in the King's interest and who could reasonably be accepted as a leader by most members of the

Council. The only such man in 1547 was the Earl of Hertford, an experienced soldier and councillor, brother of Queen Jane Seymour, and uncle to the King.

Edward Seymour was the eldest son of Sir John Seymour of Wolf Hall in Wiltshire, a knight who had served with distinction in the wars of Henry VII and Henry VIII. It would be a mistake to suppose that the family's rise to fortune and prominence came solely from Jane Seymour's marriage to the King, for Edward, who had been admitted to court on the strength of his father's military services, had attracted the King's notice and won considerable favour before Jane was in any way distinguished from the other ladies of the court. It was very probably Edward's standing in the King's favour that secured Jane's appointment as Lady in Waiting successively to each of Henry's first two queens, and it was most likely his interest in the father and son that first directed Henry's attention to the daughter. Moreover, it was not the marriage of Henry and Jane in 1536 that set the seal on the Seymours' prosperity – for the Boleyns who had risen from the gentry at Anne's marriage fell into virtual oblivion at her death – but rather the facts that Jane still held the King's affections when she died in 1537 and, above all, that she proved to be the mother of his only surviving son. With the birth of Prince Edward on 12 October, 1537, the Seymours were inalienably bound to the crown.

Old Sir John had died in the year of his daughter's royal marriage, leaving Edward, already in possession of one of the largest estates in Wiltshire, to receive full benefit from the King's gratitude. Edward Seymour, born in about 1505, is first mentioned as a page to Princess Mary (sister of Henry VIII) at her marriage in 1514 to Louis XII of France. For a time thereafter he was in the service of Cardinal Wolsey. He gained his first experience of military action when serving in the Duke of Suffolk's expedition to France, where he was knighted at Roye in November of 1523. He was a successful courtier as well as a soldier, and was appointed Master of the Horse to Henry's illegitimate son, the Duke of Richmond, in 1525. Two years later he attended Wolsey on his embassy to France and on return was successively appointed Esquire of the Royal Household, Esquire of the Body, and Gentleman of the Privy Chamber. He received grants from the King of lands in Wiltshire, Somerset, and Yorkshire, and had the privilege of lending Henry money and not getting it back again. A week after Jane's marriage on 30 May, 1536, Seymour was created Viscount Beauchamp of Hache, and at the birth of Edward in the following year he was further advanced as Earl of Hertford. In May of 1537 he was appointed to the Privy Council.

Hertford's tenure of royal favour was not adversely affected either by the death of Queen Jane or by the fall of Thomas Cromwell, with whose reforming Protestantism he sympathised and to whom he was related by the marriage of his sister Elizabeth to Cromwell's son. In January, 1541, he was made a Knight of the Garter and in the next two years held successively the offices of Warden of the Scottish Marches, Lord High Admiral, and Lord Great Chamberlain. When war broke out in 1543 Hertford was given command of the forces sent against the Scots, and was successful to the extent of sacking Edinburgh in May, 1544. In August he was transferred to Boulogne where an English force was holding out against the French, and early in the next year he routed the opposing forces. In September of 1545 he was again leading punitive raids against the Scots, who had somewhat retrieved their position since his departure for France, and in 1546 he was back at Boulogne where he eventually concluded a peace with the French. The wars of 1543–1546 added considerably to Hertford's prestige and popularity, for where he led the English were successful whereas other commanders frequently suffered reverses.

At the time of Henry's death the Earl of Hertford was an experienced statesman, a trusted councillor of ten years' standing, the country's most distinguished soldier, and the young King's closest male relative. His proposal that Paget, the Secretary of State, should help him to the Protectorate was not unreasonable.

Henry left his realm outwardly at peace and enjoying apparent domestic stability, but in reaching their decision outside Henry's death chamber Hertford and Paget must have considered several latent problems which any weakness in the central administration would rapidly bring into the open. Political differences with the Scots remained unresolved, and at home loomed two divisive issues which could easily cause both dissension in the Council and disaffection in the country. First, although Henry had achieved a definite separation of the English church from the Roman, he had left unsettled the urgent question of whether and to what extent the doctrines of the English church should depart from those of Catholicism. Secondly, this state of doctrinal uncertainty was combining with circumstances of unusual economic hardship in many parts of the countryside to produce serious popular discontent. The strength of Henry's personality and the efficiency of his control had so far held both these problems in check. While he lived it was generally accepted that the doctrine of the English church would be whatever Henry thought it should be, and although there had been popular uprisings – the Pilgrimage of Grace in 1536 and the further northern disturbances of 1537 – at no point had Henry's government been seriously threatened by widespread disaffection. But the old King's death raised at once the question of reform or conservation in religion and, if the central administration showed any sign of weakness or hesitancy, opened the way to the forcible expression of popular discontent.

Since the execution of Queen Catherine Howard in February, 1542, Henry had inclined increasingly to religious reform. The strongest of the Catholics were Catherine's uncle, Thomas Howard, Duke of Norfolk, and Stephen Gardiner, Bishop of Winchester. In Henry's last months Gardiner had been dropped from favour and Norfolk arrested for complicity in the foolish treason of his son, the Earl of Surrey. The reforming Protestants, led by Hertford and backed by the influence of Queen Catherine Parr, were clearly in the ascendant when Henry died, but his demise might have removed the basis for their political predominance. The new Council included several powerful Catholics, notably Lord Chancellor Wriothesley, and Gardiner was still a force to be reckoned with even though Henry had deliberately left his name off the list of executors of the royal will. Norfolk, moreover, remained problematically alive in the Tower, saved from following his son to the block by the King's death only hours before the sentence was to be carried out. Quick and concerted action by leading Catholics on the news of Henry's passing could conceivably have secured Norfolk's release and established a strong faction opposed to the reforms to which Cranmer, Hertford, and many of the populace were looking forward. By such considerations as these Paget was no doubt impelled to take swift and secret action to ensure Hertford's immediate installation in the seat of government.

Henry's death was at first known to only a few besides Paget and Hertford. Cranmer and Denny were present and were both doubtless made party to the plan at once, for they successfully concealed the news for three days. Parliament, which should have been dissolved automatically at the sovereign's demise, met illegally on Saturday, 29 January, and learnt the truth only on the following Monday morning from the Lord Chancellor. Meanwhile Paget and Hertford moved to implement their decision. The Earl set out, only an hour or so after the King had died, to bring Edward from the town of Hertford back to London, which they entered together, amidst general acclamation, after the news had been made public on the following Monday. Paget in the meantime, armed with possession of the late King's will, spoke to other councillors to secure their support. When the new Council met for the first time on the afternoon of Monday, 31 January, in the Tower of London, there was little protest, and no sustained resistance, in the face of Hertford's seizure of sole power. In creating a Protectorate the Council followed the precedent set at the death of Henry V in 1422 when the new King's uncles, John, Duke of Bedford, and Humphry, Duke of Gloucester, were made Protectors of the realm during the minority of Henry VI. Neither Protectorate long succeeded in averting conflict.

The Council had not, by this act, intended altogether to resign the powers and functions assigned it under Henry's will. Hertford had secured Paget's support only by promising him a virtual partnership in matters of policy, and the remaining councillors were no doubt led to expect that Hertford would govern, to a greater extent than had kings in living memory, by the advice of the Council. The justification for the Protectorate, however, lay in the need for strong personal rule, and it was probably inevitable that Hertford should, in the event, give less heed to the Council than the councillors thought proper, and so lose their trust and support.

In a ceremony held at the Tower on February 17, designed to demonstrate the unity of the Council, to enhance its prestige, and to create a number of powerful supporters of its authority, several peerages were conferred and high offices of state distributed. The peerages were supposedly awarded in accord with the late King's intentions, intentions expressed to Paget whose word was now accepted as sufficient authority. The unity of the Council was suggested by the promotion of Lord Wriothesley, from whom opposition to Hertford might have been expected, to the earldom of Southampton. In the event, however, opposition was to come from John Dudley, Viscount Lisle, on this day created Earl of Warwick, who within three years overthrew the Lord Protector. Five peerages were awarded outside the Council. William Parr, Earl of Essex and brother to the dowager Queen Catherine, became Marquess of Northampton. Sir Richard Rich, Sir William Willoughby, Sir Edmund Sheffield, and Sir Thomas Seymour (the Protector's brother) were made barons. The highest honour went naturally to Hertford himself, who became Duke of Somerset. Warwick succeeded Hertford as Lord Great Chamberlain, and was in turn succeeded as Lord High Admiral by Sir Thomas Seymour, now Lord Seymour of Sudeley. Somerset took the offices of High Treasurer and Earl Marshal formerly held by the Duke of Norfolk. Five of these eight peers, Northampton, Warwick, Willoughby, Sheffield, and Somerset, were to be prominent in the events of Kett's rebellion.

Three days later, on Sunday, 20 February, the young King was crowned at Westminster. The formalities were complete and a new reign had begun.

2. *Economic Problems*

The causes of the Norfolk rebellion, and of most of the civil disturbances of 1548–1549, were economic and social rather than political. In some parts of the country the government's religious policies were contested, as in the west and in the Pilgrimage of Grace thirteen years before, but religious doctrine was not a factor in the eastern rising. The trouble lay largely in the gradual transition which was taking place between the manorial system of local economy, in which each village was a self-sustaining agricultural unit wherein every member, from the lord to the poorest cottager, had certain rights, certain duties, and a reasonable guarantee of subsistence, to a capitalist economy in which the unit is the individual landowner who decides his own policies with the object of getting maximum return from his property. The term which covers most aspects of this transition is "enclosure", but the forms which enclosure might take were many and varied. Some forms of enclosure could be generally beneficial, for under most circumstances there is no doubt that it resulted in higher yield from the land involved. Many forms of enclosure, however, caused serious hardship among the commons who were thereby deprived of rights which had been theirs under the manorial system, and who in some cases lost their lands altogether.

A harmless and generally profitable form of enclosure had been practised in England for well over a century before the rebellion. By general agreement the landowners of a manor would redistribute their holdings so that, instead of each having one or more strips in each of the great fields of the manor, each would have a consolidated holding which he could then enclose and farm in his own way. Enclosed fields were farmed by their owners independently of other farmers: they were no longer part of a communal system which obliged every man to farm according to a general plan and to open his land to common grazing at certain times of the year. Enclosure of this sort almost always meant increased productivity and, from the point of view of the individual farmer, greater efficiency and higher profits. Once the principle of enclosure was recognised, however, it did not stop short at mere redistribution of holdings. Once there was seen to be profit in the amalgamation of strips the enterprising farmer sought not only to consolidate the lands which were his under the manorial system but also to acquire more land from the commons or from his neighbours. Many yeoman farmers evidently did find means to rent or purchase increasing tracts of land as the old manorial structure began slowly to crumble, but none was in a better position for this undertaking than the lord, who already (unless he or his predecessors had alienated it) held the demesne farm and from whom all other lands in the manor were held.

Tenure of lands within the manor was of several kinds, broadly classifiable as freehold, copyhold, leasehold, and tenure by will of the lord. Freehold tenures were secure, as were leaseholds within the term of the lease. Copyhold tenures varied considerably in nature according to manorial customs. At law the copyhold tenant usually had as strong a security as the freeholder, but the peculiarities of his position could expose him to pressures which might prevent him from asserting his legal rights: in times of economic hardship the lords may in many cases have been able to apply such pressures to drive their poorer copyhold tenants off their lands. Tenure by will means more or less what it says, and lands so held could be resumed by the lord at any time. Historians following R. H. Tawney have probably exaggerated the extent of these evictions; but there were certainly cases in the sixteenth century of copyholders and tenants at will being dispossessed in order that their lands might be enclosed, and such cases became a source of popular grievance against enclosing landlords.[1]

Enclosure which went beyond the redistribution of holdings within the manor caused hardship to the poorer commons. Even those who were not deprived of their lands faced serious losses of rights on the manorial lands, for as more land was enclosed less was available for common grazing. Many, by fair means or foul, were deprived of lands altogether, and a new class, that of the landless labourer, was thus created. This in itself would not have been problematic if a balance had been preserved such that those who no longer occupied lands themselves were able to find employment on the lands of others, but such a balance was not preserved, primarily because of the sheep.

With the rise of the English cloth industry the breeding of sheep for wool had become increasingly profitable, and nowhere more so than in East Anglia, where cloth manufacture was the major industry of Norwich and many of the surrounding villages. Throughout the fifteenth century and through the first half of the sixteenth the production of wool increased as English cloth found better and better markets abroad. The old manorial system, however, was not easily adapted to the large-scale raising of flocks: the best profits went to those who farmed large enclosed tracts where sheep could be raised with minimal overheads. The desire to embark on large-scale sheep farming was not the only motive towards enclosure but it was a common one and one which aroused particular resentment, for when large areas of land were converted to pasture there was no longer employment on that land for the labourer: where dozens of men had once been required for tillage two or three shepherds could now manage alone. The landlord increased his profits but many landless labourers, now without homes or employment, cast angry eyes on the new pastures which had once guaranteed their livelihood. Enclosure by larger landlords was generally unpopular, but enclosure for the specific purpose of raising sheep was bitterly resented by the poor because the flocks not only occupied land which had once been theirs but also rendered their labours cheap or unwanted.

Several Norfolk families rose to considerable riches through their flocks. The Fermors of East Barsham had some 17,000 sheep in the county in 1521, income from which enabled them to build the beautiful manor house which still stands. (When Sir William Fermor died in 1557 without children his lands and flocks were inherited by his nephew, son of his brother Thomas who had been killed by the rebels on Rising Chase.) Sir Richard Southwell of Woodrising, who was active in the suppression of Kett's rebellion, had over 13,000 sheep in 1551. An indication of the rate at which the flocks were growing in Norfolk comes from the Townshend records: Sir Roger Townshend of Raynham in 1544 owned three thousand sheep in the county (held by his son Thomas who married Southwell's granddaughter Anne), but in 1548 he had 4,200.[2] Another family whose fortunes rose largely through the conversion of their lands to sheep runs were the Heydons of Baconsthorpe and Saxlingham. Sir John Heydon (died 1550) made his castle at Baconsthorpe the centre of an extensive local woollen industry, and his successor, Sir Christopher (died 1579), is said to have entertained at Christmas no less than thirty head shepherds employed to oversee his flocks.

The riots and rebellions of the 1540s were most frequently directed against the enclosed pastures. The Norfolk rebels in particular began by pulling down fences, and included in their list of demands several which aimed specifically at the limitation of sheep farming. Their hostility to sheep was demonstrated when, in their period of power on Mousehold Heath, they destroyed many thousands of the animals. Among the first to go were the flocks of Thomas Bacon (brother to Nicholas who was to be Lord Keeper under Elizabeth) which were pastured on the heathland outside Norwich. After the rebellion Sir Thomas Wodehouse of Waxham complained that the rebels had butchered two thousand of his sheep. Considerable irony, however, lies in the fact that the rebellions of 1549 were protesting against economic movements which, as can be seen in retrospect, were all but over by that time. The main wave of enclosures is now estimated to have occurred between 1440 and 1520: by 1549 the process of enclosure for pasture had slowed considerably and may even have reached a standstill. The English woollen industry itself reached its peak about two years later, and thereafter, because of changes in the international market, began a long decline from which it was never to recover. By the mid-sixteenth century, therefore, the profits to be gained from sheep had reached their peak, and with them also the immediate profits to be gained from enclosure.

The peasant of 1549 could not know this, and to have done so would not have improved his condition. He was, moreover, faced with other problems besides the fences and the sheep, for since the late fifteenth-century England, like most of Europe, had experienced a slow but steady inflation of prices. At a very rough estimate the prices of most commodities in 1549 were double what they had been in 1500. Had this rise occurred steadily, at a rate of about two per cent per annum, it would hardly have been troublesome, but the records indicate that the rate of inflation had increased sharply since about 1543 and remained abnormally high with no sign of levelling.[3] The reasons are hard to discover with certainty, but the expense of England's foreign wars, begun towards the end of Henry's reign, was surely a major factor. To finance them the government sold Crown lands (fortunately plentiful after the confiscation of monastic properties) and debased the coinage. The sale of Crown lands made no immediate difference to the peasant, but debasement of the currency contributed to the domestic inflation. The small farmer and the labourer were not only being forced off the land but were also facing what was for them an unprecedented rate of increase in the cost of living. Successive debasement, begun by Henry to finance his Scottish wars, continued under Somerset and Northumberland. Only towards the end of Edward's reign did England's position in international markets become so acutely embarrassed that reform of the currency was at last undertaken. Sir Thomas Gresham, who as a Norfolk gentleman plays some part in the story of the rebellion, then emerged as the financial advisor behind this reform and was largely responsible for the ultimate restoration of foreign confidence.

To many contemporaries the problems of inflation and enclosure seemed connected. It was argued that the profits of sheep farming created a demand for land and, at the same time, decreased the proportion of land under tillage, and thus created food shortages and rising prices. The solution then seemed obvious: rigid restrictions should be placed on sheep farming and enclosures in order to preserve the balance of the old manorial economy. A number of learned and articulate men in Somerset's day were expounding this argument. They included influential preachers such as Hugh Latimer and members of Parliament like John Hales, and were called "Commonwealth Men" because their ideal was a Christian state dedicated to the common good. The chief texts of the movement are to be found in Latimer's sermons and in the *Discourse of the Common Weal of the Realm of England* which was probably written in the autumn of 1549 perhaps by Hales himself.[4]

Somerset was inclined to accept the argument that agrarian problems, and the conversion of tillage to pasture in particular, were responsible for inflation. He accepted it not so much because he shared the ideals of the Commonwealth Men – although he may to some extent have done so – as because the alternative explanation (offered at the time by Sir Thomas Smith and others) indicated the government's own debasement of the coinage as the source of the trouble. Somerset must have seen the force of this alternative argument, but he could not accept it officially because debasement was necessary to finance the government's current military undertakings in Scotland, to the prosecution of which Somerset and the Council were fully committed.[5] Accordingly the Council addressed itself to the remedy of the agrarian problems, and Somerset himself became a firm believer in the virtue of official commissions sent out into the countryside to examine complaints and provide the information upon which legislative reforms in the near future should be based.

The situation is a network of ironies. Kett and his followers rebelled against a government led by one who evidently agreed with the substance of their demands; and in rebelling, although they failed, they did indirectly cause the downfall of that government. Somerset, moreover, was not adopting new or controversial policies, but following precedents laid down in the two previous reigns. Tudor kings traditionally sided with the commons against the landowners on agrarian matters, and commissions of inquiry had been employed with some success many years before by Wolsey. But whereas the kings had tended to let the statutes against enclosures lie idle Somerset proposed to enforce them, and in promising such reform he created the civil commotion which, by tacitly avoiding reform, the Tudors had usually averted.

The kings had supported the peasantry and the manorial economy for political reasons. The manor was not only an agricultural unit but also a political and military one. The lord of the manor held his land ultimately from the King, and in return supplied man-power from his tenantry to make up the royal armies in time of war. It was therefore in the royal interest to maintain a high proportion of the land under tillage rather than pasture, for a manor devoted to pasture could best be managed by a steward and a handful of shepherds whereas the same lands farmed in the traditional way would require a full complement of labourers and artisans. The depopulation of areas devoted to pasture threatened the security of a nation which still maintained no standing army but relied on a militia in times of war. The Tudors therefore passed Acts at regular intervals prohibiting enclosures, rural depopulation, and conversion of arable land to pasture, the earliest being that of 1489 and the latest, prior to the Protectorate, those of 1534 and 1536. In 1517 Wolsey had instituted a commission to enquire into the state of enclosures in the counties of Oxfordshire, Buckinghamshire, Northamptonshire, Berkshire, and Warwickshire, with a view to enforcing these statutes, and as a result had ordered restitution for all enclosures made since 1485.

Somerset's agrarian policy was a determined continuation of that which had been sporadically applied for over half a century, but in carrying out his plans the Duke defeated the expectations of both the commons and the gentry. The gentry naturally thought that Somerset, himself a large landowner, would not enforce an agrarian policy which favoured the peasant at the expense of the landlord, whereas the commons, it seems, knowing Somerset's intentions, construed the inevitable delays in the process of reform as signs of obstruction from the local landlords and therefore felt justified in taking matters into their own hands. Kett's men believed in all sincerity that they were enforcing the law against corrupt local officials and confidently expected not only backing but even payment from Somerset's administration. But Somerset could not condone the rebellions, which in the event gave the lords the evidence they needed to condemn and prevent Somerset's policies.

3. *The Protector's Policies*

In the two and a half years between his assumption of power early in 1547 and his fall in October of 1549 the Duke of Somerset had gone a long way towards enforcing systematically the old laws against enclosures. Besides instituting a programme of agrarian reform he also showed unusual lenience towards the commons both in the judgments given by his authority in the Court of Requests and in several pardons granted to rioters guilty of throwing down enclosures. In all of these ways he aroused the hopes of the commons and the opposition of the aristocracy.

His first step was to grant in May, 1548, a petition from the tenants of Walton, Weybridge, Esher, and Shepperton, who complained that the creation of the deer park at Hampton Court in the later years of Henry VIII had deprived them of common rights essential to their livelihood. By order of the Privy Council (under Somerset's direction) the enclosures in question were removed and the ancient rights of the tenants restored. Only one estate was involved here, and since the landlord in question was the Crown no-one protested; but Somerset's action over Hampton Court park was a foreshadowing of the national policy he was to launch a few weeks later. In the same month of May, moreover, he issued a proclamation pardoning, with a few individual exceptions, a group of persons in Cornwall who had risen in rebellion in the last months of the old King's reign.[1] Cornwall was still in a restive state and was in fact to rebel again in the next year. The general feeling on the Council was that Somerset's lenience would encourage further disturbances, and it was with increasing displeasure that the gentry witnessed a succession of such pardons issued over the next few months as riots against enclosures became more and more frequent.

In June, 1548, the Protector announced his agrarian policy in another proclamation, perhaps the most important that he issued:

> Forasmuch as the King's majesty, the Lord Protector's grace, and the rest of his Privy Council, hath been advertised and put in remembrance, as well by divers supplications and pitiful complaints of his majesty's poor subjects as also by other wise and discreet men having care to the good order of the realm,

that of late by the enclosing of lands and arable grounds in divers and sundry places of this realm many have been driven to extreme poverty and compelled to leave the places where they were born and to seek them livings in other countries, with great misery and poverty; insomuch that whereas in time past, 10, 20, yea, in some place 100 or 200 Christian people hath been inhabiting and kept household to the bringing forth and nourishing of youth and to the replenishing and fulfilling of his majesty's realms with faithful subjects who might serve both Almighty God and the King's majesty to the defense of this realm, now there is nothing kept but sheep or bullocks; all that land which heretofore was tilled and occupied with so many men, and did bring forth not only divers families in work and labour, but also capons, hens, chickens, pigs, and other such furniture of the markets, is now gotten, by insatiable greediness of mind, into one or two men's hands and scarcely dwelled upon with one poor shepherd, so that the realm thereby is brought to a marvelous desolation, houses decayed, parishes diminished, the force of the realm weakened, and Christian people, by the greedy covetousness of some men, eaten up and devoured of brute beasts and driven from their houses by sheep and bullocks; and that although of the same thing many and sundry complaints and lamentations hath been heretofore made, and by the most wise and discreet princes, his majesty's father and grandfather, the Kings of most famous memory, King Henry VII and King Henry VIII, with the consent and assent of the lords spiritual and temporal in divers parliaments assembled, divers and sundry laws and acts of parliaments and most godly ordinances in their several times hath been made for the remedy thereof, yet the insatiable covetousness of men doth not cease daily to encroach hereupon and more and more to waste the realm, after this sort bringing arable grounds into pastures, and letting houses, whole families, and copyholds to fall down, decay, and be waste:

Wherefore his highness ... hath appointed, according to the said acts and proclamations, a view and inquiry to be made of all such as contrary to the said acts and godly ordinances hath made enclosures and pastures of that which was arable ground, or let any house, tenement, or mese decay and fall down, or otherwise committed or done anything to the contrary of the good and wholesome articles contained in the said acts.[2]

Commissioners were accordingly appointed and divided into several committees to survey different parts of the country. One of these committees, that headed by John Hales and including Sir Francis Russell, Sir Fulke Greville, John Marsh, William Pinnock, and Roger Amys, actually went into operation in the summer of 1548, its appointed area being the counties of Oxfordshire, Buckinghamshire, Berkshire, Warwickshire, Leicestershire, Bedfordshire, and Northamptonshire. The object was to produce a general survey on the information of which the next parliamentary session might proceed to redressive legislation. Information on specific cases was to be sent to the Court of Chancery where proceedings might then be instituted against offenders. Very little was in fact achieved: only one area, the midlands, was actually surveyed, and no proceedings were taken in Chancery.

The commissions, actual and projected, of 1548, seem to have had the backing of the Council: they were certainly not (unlike those of the next year) instituted on Somerset's sole authority. The government supported inquiry into agrarian problems because as we have seen, the conversion of tillage to pasture was generally blamed both for the high rate of inflation and for depopulation of rural areas. Throughout these years Somerset was directing a war in Scotland the continuation of which required that sheep, and not debasement, be blamed for inflation, and that there be a steady supply of manpower. The commissions had the advantage of at once addressing the economic crisis without hindering the war effort and of promising to remedy the rural depopulation which was blamed for England's military weakness. At this stage, in the summer of 1548, Somerset was by no means alone in his faith in the enclosure commissions.[3]

Only one committee began its work, and even this one suspended its operations over the autumn and winter of 1548, probably because Hales, its chairman, had business in Parliament. Hales sat as member for Preston, and in this, the second Edwardian Parliament, he introduced no less than three Bills for agrarian reform. The first required the rebuilding of decayed houses and the maintenance of a proper proportion of land under tillage, the second forbade speculation on foodstuffs, and the third encouraged cattle breeding in place of sheep grazing. None of these was passed into law. Hales' committee returned to work in the summer of 1549 but found its task hindered by the great insurrections, and soon after terminated by the fall of the Protectorate. Hales was so closely identified with Somerset's by then controversial policies that he went into voluntary exile on the Continent until the accession of Elizabeth.

Hales' Bills failed to pass into law, not so much because of their content as because of the character and rhetoric of Hales himself, which seem to have aroused general antagonism.[4] Somerset succeeded, in the same session, in passing the Subsidy Act in March, 1549, an Act intended to raise revenue by means of a tax on personal property at the rate of one shilling in the pound, and by a special tax on sheep. This Act has traditionally been regarded as part of the agrarian policy which manifested itself also in the enclosure commissions of 1548 and 1549, but it is probable that its primary purpose was simply to raise revenue. It would have been largely ineffective as a punitive measure against sheep farmers.[5] In any event, Somerset was in the Tower before the tax fell due.

In the same month as the passage of the Subsidy Act the Protector secured passage of a private Act which in effect granted a measure of security of tenure to copyholders on his own estates. This Act too has been seen as part of Somerset's wider, liberal agrarian policy, but it is more likely to have stemmed from motives of simple charity or from the desire for good repute which Somerset, as a national leader in difficult times, wisely pursued wherever convenient. The effect of the private Act was negligible and cost Somerset very little.[6]

In May, 1549, he issued another general proclamation enforcing the old statutes against enclosures and concluding with a threat:

> Or else if gentleness will not now provoke and cause that thing be amended which duty should do and laws may compel: his highness, of his most royal duty and love, which his majesty beareth to this his region and country and to the maintenance of the manred thereof, is fully minded from henceforth, by advice aforesaid, to put in ure all the said penal laws heretofore made for the repressing of such offences, and straightly to see them executed against all such as shall be found culpable, without pardon or remission.[7]

A proclamation of May 23, on the other hand, takes note that "certain numbers of disobedient and seditious persons, assembling themselves together unlawfully in some parts of the realm, have most arrogantly and disloyally, under pretense of the said proclamation [i.e. that of April, 1549, just quoted], taken upon them his majesty's authority, presumed to pluck his highness' sword out of his hand, and so gone about to chastise and correct whom they thought good, in plucking down pales, hedges, and ditches at their will and pleasure."[8] The riots of 1549 had begun in earnest and Somerset was torn between the will to implement his agrarian reforms and the need to maintain civil order. The proclamation goes on to state that steps have already been taken to remedy abuses and that riotous disorder will be met and punished by force of arms. A proclamation of June 14, however, pardoned those rioters who had "humbly submitted themselves" because "this outrage was done rather of folly and mistaking the said proclamation [again that of April] ... than of malice or any evil will."[9] The admission that the proclamations against enclosures were at least in part responsible for the social unrest they were designed to prevent shows clearly the dilemma of Somerset's position.

In June a commission was appointed to dispark the Crown lands in Sussex recently acquired by the forfeitures of the Duke of Norfolk and Lord Seymour of Sudeley (the Protector's brother). Early in July Somerset, on his own authority, revived the commissions of inquiry and by September Hales, with a new panel of commissioners, was again at work in the midlands. Other commissions appear to have operated in Cambridgeshire, Kent, and Sussex. These commissions, unlike those of the previous year, were given power not only to inquire and report but also to hear and determine. The idea of enclosure commissions was not original to Somerset's administration, and neither was Somerset by any means alone in seeing them as a promising remedy to agrarian discontent. The commissions of 1548 appear to have had the general consent of the Council, but many of those who had at first endorsed them began to doubt the wisdom of the commissions in the light of the popular disturbances they appeared to provoke. Somerset's establishment of commissions with enlarged powers in the summer of 1549 was effected either without consulting his colleagues or in the face of their opposition. This was one of the chief objections raised by them against Somerset at his trial. It was not the method to which they objected, but the time of its application. The enclosure commissions were known to have produced riots in 1548, and the summer of 1549, when several serious outbreaks had already begun, appeared to most councillors to be no time to repeat the previous year's experiment.[10]

By that time the disorders in the countryside were spreading faster than Somerset's reforms could take effect and by July armies were already being sent against parties of rebels. The armies acted with increasing independence of Somerset whose authority, because of his admitted responsibility for the disordered state of affairs, was inevitably weakening. The Duke himself could only continue the vain attempt to restore peace by alternating threats and pardons. A proclamation of July 11 declared forfeit all properties of the rebels in Devon and Cornwall. Another issued the next day pardoned all those guilty of "riotous assembly" who had made "humble submission."[11] A proclamation of July 16 pardoned submissive rioters but threatened martial law against future offenders.[12]

Somerset's response to the rebellions was initially lenient: the heralds and lieutenants sent to confront the rioters were almost always instructed to begin by attempting to achieve dispersal with an offer of pardon. Only if promises of pardon and eventual remedy failed was military force to be used, and even then punishment was to be confined as far as possible to the ringleaders. The application of these guidelines varied considerably, for the local commanders enjoyed virtual autonomy: actual dealing with rioters ranged from the paternalistic reasonings of the Earl of Arundel to the swift capital reprisals of Sir William Herbert. Somerset's policy of lenience was dictated by the situation. In the first place he cannot but have recognized the justice of the claims of those who were protesting against enclosures, for it was current government policy to blame these same abuses for England's inflationary and military difficulties. The very appointment of further commissions in July was a tacit acknowledgment that there existed abuses to be remedied. Secondly, preoccupied as he was with the need for men and money to fight his northern war Somerset would not have wanted to alienate – much less to massacre – the peasantry from whose ranks his soldiers were to be drawn. Thirdly, and on account of the same preoccupation, Somerset tried to avoid military confrontations at home in order to be able to deploy maximal forces against the Scots. On the other hand, Somerset could not, and did not wish to, tolerate rebellion. Although he admitted a degree of justice in the rebel cause, and although political circumstances required that he deal with them more gently than many of his colleagues would otherwise have wished, the Protector had no intention of abetting insurgents.

At Somerset's trial his lenience towards the rebels was interpreted as sympathy for them and used against him. Overall this accusation was a gross distortion, for Somerset's policy towards the rebellions had been largely dictated by circumstances recognized and to some extent created by the Council as a whole, but it contained an uncomfortable grain of truth in that the Protector's enthusiasm for enclosure commissions was undeniably responsible for augmenting the riots and in that his initial lenience towards the rebels had the effect of encouraging the rebellions.[13]

Had Somerset been able to take a firm stand against the rioters from the beginning it is possible that the more serious outbreaks of 1549 would not have occurred. He was, moreover, forced to admit, as in the proclamation of May 23, that his own reforms were in part to blame for the disorders, and he was therefore doubly prevented from the kind of decisive military action advocated by Warwick and Herbert. When no alternative to armed force remained Somerset's authority was so far undermined, and his policies so discredited, that the commanders in the field had become the actual arbitars of the situation. Somerset could hardly continue to lead the country in carrying out repressive measures, of which he was known to disapprove, against rebels with whom he was thought to sympathize. His overthrow was postponed until October, 1549, more than a month after the rebellions had been crushed, but it was politically inevitable from the moment that large-scale military action against the rebels became necessary.

Somerset could not put down the rebellion b/c they were acting in accordance w/ Royal Proclamations.

4. *Wymondham*

The Priory of St. Mary and St. Alban was founded at Wymondham by William d'Albini, Chief Butler to Henry I, in 1107. The buildings for the accommodation of a Prior and twelve Benedictine monks were completed in about 1130. Some time after the death of Archbishop Thomas Becket in 1172 the Priory was rededicated to St. Mary and St. Thomas. St. Thomas of Canterbury was further honoured in Wymondham by the foundation in 1172 of the chapel in Church Street in which two monks were installed to pray for the souls of the Archbishop and of the founder's family. The founder of the chapel was William d'Albini, Earl of Arundel, son of the founder of the Priory. The Earl of Arundel, who had married Adeliza of Louvain, widow of Henry I, also founded at Westwode in the manor of Choseley near the northwest road from Wymondham a cell of the order of St. Lazarus of Jerusalem, known as the Westwode Chapel. The Master and the two or three brethren of this chapel were to offer prayers for the souls of King Stephen, Queen Matilda, and Queen Adeliza (the founder's wife). This Earl of Arundel was also the builder of the castles at New Buckenham and Castle Rising.

Apart from the great castle at Rising little of substance remains of these twelfth-century d'Albini foundations. The present Abbey Church at Wymondham covers only half the ground occupied by the original Priory and associated buildings, and most of the visible exterior today is of the fifteenth century or later. From within, however, the twelfth-century nave, only half the length of the old church, gives an idea of the style of the Abbey, and the foundations and chapter house arch which can still be found to the east of the ruined octagon tower suggest its original extent. The chapel of St. Thomas, wholly rebuilt in the late fourteenth century, served for many years after the dissolution as a school and has more recently been used as a county library. The Westwode Chapel has disappeared, except for the foundations which can still be traced. Buckenham Castle remained standing until the mid-seventeenth century when its fortifications were demolished, presumably to prevent its use as a royalist stronghold during the civil wars. These twelfth-century d'Albini foundations are, outside the city of Norwich and its immediate environs, the chief sites associated with Kett's rebellion.

The most striking features of Wymondham Abbey are its two towers, the late fourteenth-century eastern octagonal tower, disused since the dissolution, and the mid-fifteenth-century square tower at the west end. The two towers are emblems of over three hundred years of dissension between the Abbey and the town of Wymondham, a quarrel the effects of which survived the dissolution to become one of the roots of the rebellion which began in Wymondham in 1549.

The Priory church was also the parish church of Wymondham and from early in the thirteenth century there were disputes over the building between the monks and the townspeople, between the Prior and the Vicar.[1] Strife at Wymondham was bitter enough in 1249 to require an appeal to Rome, in response to which came a Bull from Innocent IV dividing the church between the two parties. The townspeople were assigned the parish church, which was to consist of the nave, the north aisle, and the northwest tower. (The church originally had two low towers flanking the west front, evidence for which can still be seen in the pillars of the first bay of the nave.) The monks were assigned the choir, the transepts, the south aisle, and the southwest tower. Such an arrangement could be satisfactory only with the goodwill of those involved, which appears to have been wanting on both sides. Serious disagreement broke out a century and a half later when the monks moved the bells from the central tower to the northwest tower, which belonged to the parishioners, and began rebuilding what is now the eastern octagonal tower. In so doing they constructed a thick wall completely filling the western arch of the central tower, which may not have encroached upon the area of the parish church but which considerably diminished its apparent size by totally blocking the view from the nave into the choir. When the tower was completed, moreover, and the bells returned to their former place, the monks sealed the access from the townspeople so that no other bells could be installed or rung from the central tower. Disturbances followed, and in 1409 an appeal from the Prior, William Roydon, resulted in the parish churchwardens being bound over on penalty of £100 each to keep the peace. But the trouble continued in the following year when several minor assaults on Priory personnel culminated in an attack led by one Roger Plumer in which Prior Roydon was held prisoner for two days in the southwest tower. By this time the parishioners had placed their own bells in the northwest tower and had blocked up the doors by which the Prior could, by right as Parson of the church, enter the parishioners' section of the building. The Prior appealed to the Exchequer Court, and Lord Chancellor Beaufort appointed a commission of local gentry to examine the matter in

1411. Appeal on behalf of the convent was also made directly to the King, Henry IV, who sent Thomas Arundel, the Archbishop of Canterbury, to conclude a settlement at Wymondham. Arundel allowed the parishioners to retain their bells in the northwest tower on condition that they used them only on proper occasions and did not disturb the monks' hours of rest. The parishioners then felt that a more substantial, loftier tower was needed to house the parish bells and, planning to build one as an extension to the west end, they began to demolish the old west porch to make way for it. As this was possibly not within their rights under the various settlements the Prior took proceedings and obtained an injunction to prevent the continuation of their work. In the 1440s, however, Sir John Clifton of Buckenham Castle, by diplomacy and benefactions, persuaded the Prior to permit the building: and so was built the west tower of Wymondham Abbey from which William Kett was hanged a century later.

In the four years between 1536 and 1540 Henry VIII, through the agency of Thomas Cromwell, achieved the dissolution of every remaining monastic institution in the realm. Wymondham Abbey fell in 1539, and the old question of the parishioners' rights over the church building was reopened after almost a century of concord. When the Abbey was dissolved its lands, revenues, buildings, and plate became Crown property. The buildings were to be demolished and the materials, especially the stone from the walls and the lead from the roofs, collected and sold. To oversee the demolition and removal of materials the Crown appointed a local agent, Sir John Flowerdew, a Sergeant at Law who owned lands at Hethersett and who resided, at least for a time, at Stanfield Hall nearby. The parishioners, who may already have felt mistrust or disapprobation of Flowerdew, realized that they might well be put to the expense of patching what remained of their church after the Sergeant had removed whatever was of value in the Abbey structure. They also realized that they should not plead the rights granted them by Innocent IV against the claims of King Henry, who was notoriously unimpressed, in later life, by papal decrees. They therefore petitioned Henry that, in return for due payment, he should permit them to retain parts of the Abbey church for their use, asking in particular for those sections which shared common fabric with the parish church, namely, the central tower and the south aisle. They also requested the choir, the Lady Chapel, and the chapel of St. Thomas in the town. In 1540 the King granted the petition, but Flowerdew, who may have been appropriating the materials to his own use – or was perhaps genuinely uncertain how much of the building the King required him to despoil – continued his work of demolition, angering the townspeople who saw him removing materials which they had paid the King to let stand. (According to Blomefield, Flowerdew removed the lead from the south aisle and part of the central tower, and took stone from the south transept, the Lady Chapel, and the choir.) When the Norfolk rebellion began as a small riot in Wymondham Flowerdew was one of the first victims of resentment. The move against Flowerdew on July 8 was the last manifestation of the three hundred year old struggle of the people of Wymondham to maintain their rights over the Abbey church.

The leader of the parishioners in the movement to preserve the church fabric from Flowerdew's depredations was Robert Kett, a local farmer and the largest resident landlord in Wymondham. He is described as a tanner, which probably means not that he personally carried on that trade but that he held the manorial rights of tanning for Wymondham.[2] The Ketts, whose name appears variously as *Kett, Ket, Cat, Chat,* and *Knight,* had been landowners in Hevingham, Norfolk, since the time of King John. Their presence in Wymondham is recorded as far back as the late twelfth century.[3] The inquest held in the Guildhall at Norwich on 13 January, 1550, showed Robert Kett's property to include lands formerly belonging to the Hospital of Burton Lazars in Leicestershire, which had been granted to the Order of St. Lazarus by William d'Albini, Earl of Arundel, when he founded the Westwode Chapel in 1146, and given, after the dissolution, to the Earl of Warwick, from whom they were purchased by Kett in 1546. The Westwode Chapel itself had also passed to Warwick by Royal grant, and was purchased in 1545 by Robert Kett's brother William, who also purchased the manor of Choseley in which the chapel lies.

Robert Kett's attachment to the local church is suggested by his having named one of his younger sons Loye after Loye (or Eligius) Ferrers, the last Abbot of Wymondham who, having apparently concurred in the Supremacy, became Vicar of Wymondham on the dissolution.[4] Flowerdew was disliked in Wymondham not because he despoiled monasteries and profited from the dissolution – the Ketts themselves were ready enough to purchase former monastic properties and to put the ancient buildings to their own uses – but because, like the mediaeval priors, he threatened the very fabric of the parish church. Tradition has it that Robert Kett was already established as a leader of the townspeople in their efforts to preserve the church against Flowerdew long before the riots of July, 1549. The roots of what grew into the great rebellion reach back through several centuries of popular struggle to preserve the parish church of Wymondham for the people's use.

By 1549 the monastic foundations of the twelth-century

d'Albinis were in decidedly secular hands. St. Thomas' Chapel had been sold by the King to the town of Wymondham. The Westwode Chapel and associated lands had been granted to Warwick and purchased from him by the Ketts. The Abbey itself was granted in 1543 to Henry Howard, Earl of Surrey, but when Surrey was executed four years later it reverted to the Crown. The Howards had also obtained Castle Rising, but this too was forfeit in 1547.[5] Buckenham Castle had passed through Sir John Clifton's heiress Elizabeth to her great-great-great-grandson Sir Edmund Knyvett, who was to use it as a base against Kett's army.

5. *Civil Unrest*

Almost from the time of his death in 1172 St. Thomas Becket had been an important saint in Wymondham where there was both a priory dedicated to him and a chapel where perpetual prayers were offered for his soul. The feast of the Translation of St. Thomas on July 7 was traditionally celebrated in Wymondham with a play or pageant and with gatherings for feasting and for worship. To join in these festivities would come not only the people of Wymondham but also those from the many small towns and villages within a convenient distance. The occasion was not only for devotion and indulgence but also for meetings and the exchange of news. The gathering of people for the feast of St. Thomas at Wymondham in 1549 was the beginning of Kett's rebellion.

The disturbance which began in Wymondham and, under Kett's leadership, progressed to the seizure of Norwich was not the first manifestation of popular discontent in the summer of 1549, although it was to prove the most serious. Both in Norfolk and throughout England there were other risings varying in the numbers of persons involved, in the extent of the areas affected, and in the time and degree of force needed to put them down. These risings were connected in that they all occurred within a few months and all had, in varying proportions, the same two or three causes: desire for agrarian reform, religious discontentment, and popular hatred of the gentry. The risings were not, however, connected by any plan or general organization: each one occurred more or less spontaneously and only in a few cases is there any evidence of co-operation between rebellious persons in different areas. Had this not been the case, and had the summer risings of 1549 been co-ordinated to occur simultaneously with a common political goal, the country would almost certainly have been plunged into a protracted civil war.

The risings of 1549 did not directly bring about Somerset's fall, in so far as forces acting nominally under his authority succeeded in restoring order by the end of August, but the risings were nonetheless instrumental in the subsequent change of government in that they served to unite the Council and the aristocracy behind Warwick in opposition to the domestic policies of the Protector.

Somerset's foreign policy had also proven spectacularly unsuccessful by 1549, but this by itself had no great effect on his political position at home. The foreign dealings of Henry VIII were frequently disastrous, but the King's strength and popularity in England were, if anything, increased by reverses abroad, which could be attributed popularly to the malice of a common enemy. Somerset's foreign policies were, indeed, generally continuations of those adopted in the latter years of Henry VIII. In his handling of domestic affairs, however, the Protector aroused increasing opposition because of his persistent use of enclosure commissions which his colleagues were inclined to view as a dangerous expedient in the summer of 1549. His policy proved doubly disastrous. First, it led the commons to expect official sympathy for their demands and sanction for their actions, and so brought about the very state of popular insurgence which it was designed to obviate, and secondly, the occurrence of the risings served Warwick and the Council as evident symptoms of the failure of Somerset's domestic policy. The opposition to Somerset which united under Warwick in the autumn of 1549 had other causes – the Protector's personal aloofness, his disregard of other members of the Council, his failings in foreign policy – but no single factor gave Warwick more power than Somerset's failure to deal decisively with popular discontent, and no single manifestation of such discontent lent more to Warwick's prestige than the Norfolk rebellion which he in person suppressed.

To appreciate the wider political significance of the Norfolk rising and to discover the distinguishing features which made Kett's rebellion a matter of national importance we must consider it in the context of the general discontent which became most evident in the summer of 1549. Rebellions and treasonous plots were not uncommon in the Tudor period, a time of fundamental and relatively swift changes in the social, economic, and religious institutions of the country. Only a dozen years before a series of rebellions in the north of England, involving the leading nobility and the Archbishop of York, had caught Henry off balance and forced him to sell his plate to raise an army and, for a time at least, to treat with the rebel leaders and make concessions. This was the so-called Pilgrimage of Grace, eventually punished so ruthlessly, under Henry's orders, by the Duke of Norfolk. Again, within five years of Kett's rebellion, Sir Thomas Wyatt and other gentlemen led a rising in Kent against Queen Mary; and twenty years later still, in the reign of Elizabeth, there was another serious rising of the northern earls. The year 1549 is distinguished, with respect to its rebellions, from 1536–7, 1553–4, and 1569, by the multitude of risings which occurred, by the spread of active discontent through almost all parts of

England, and by the fact that these risings received no leadership or support from the nobility or senior gentry. The rebellions of 1549 stand apart from other internal disturbances with which successive Tudor monarchs were confronted by virtue of their origins in widespread, unplanned, uncoordinated, popular discontent.

The effort to keep order by proclamations comprising a diplomatic mixture of threats and promises shows that the Council was aware of the unsettled state of the populace well before the summer of 1549. There were several outbreaks of insurrection in the preceding year, which might have provided a definite warning but which might also have created an ill-founded confidence by the relative ease with which they were put down. Early in June, 1548, a small disturbance arose in Somerset, but was easily settled. Elsewhere in the west country rioters attacked the fences of the recently enclosed parks of Lord Stourton and Sir William Herbert, but were brought to order by Herbert who, on his own initiative, captured and hanged a number of offenders. The government met the situation by sending commissioners into the disaffected counties with the task of conciliating the people by a tactful blend of firmness and sympathy. A little later in the same summer there was a riot at Enfield, Middlesex, directed against the property of Sir Thomas Wroth. The matter was handled leniently, four of the men involved receiving brief prison sentences. Another small disturbance around Botley and Hamble in Hampshire was similarly settled without severe punitive measures. The most serious outbreak of 1548 was in Cornwall where, on April 6, the unpopular Archdeacon William Body was murdered by a mob under the leadership of Martin Geoffrey, priest of the parish of St. Keverne. Body himself, however, was probably the source of the trouble: there had been demonstrations against him in Penryn in the preceding year, and after his murder in 1548 the mob dispersed and took no further action. The affair was concluded by a general pardon for all but twenty-eight of those who participated in the riot, and of these no more than ten were hanged. By the end of the year it might have appeared that Somerset's policy of lenience and promise of reform was successfully coping with popular discontents. The violent reprisals taken by Sir William Herbert, however, probably represent a widespread feeling among the gentry and nobility that stronger measures were needed, a feeling that was to find fuel when riots broke out afresh and grew into rebellions in the next year.

Disorders began again in the spring of 1549. At first the government used the same measures as had successfully kept order the year before, issuing conciliatory proclamations and relying on the gentry to enforce the law in their own localities. By the end of

June, however, it was clear that the situation was dangerously out of control. Defensive measures were taken to protect the capital: on July 3 close watches were appointed in London and a little later martial law was declared and the city gates manned with artillery.[1] In the countryside Somerset reluctantly sanctioned the use of troops to oppose the major centres of rebellion. By the end of July most counties of England were witnessing some degree of disturbance, and some areas, notably the regions of Exeter and Norwich, were in the hands of the insurgents. The situation fell short of civil war only because there was little or no effective communication among the many rebel groups.

Disturbance broke out in Essex in the late spring and again in midsummer. Trouble in Kent was settled in May by Sir Thomas Wyatt, by whose orders a number of rioters were hanged. In Suffolk Sir Anthony Wingfield and other gentlemen successfully opposed several minor insurrections. In Surrey there were demonstrations against enclosures. Disorders in Leicestershire and Rutland were put down by the Marquess of Dorset. Lincolnshire was unsettled and appears to have sent some sympathizers to join Kett. There were serious riots in the region of Cambridge on July 10, when a band of about one hundred attacked enclosures in several of the villages around the city. Early in the summer trouble again confronted Sir William Herbert, who again appears to have dealt with it sharply and effectively. Disturbances in Hampshire, where no strong representative of authority appeared to oppose them, continued for some weeks. In Sussex the conciliatory policy of the Earl of Arundel eventually achieved the dispersal of rebel camps without armed confrontation. In Yorkshire several gentlemen were murdered and a number of rebels executed.[2]

Serious riots in Oxfordshire resulted in the assembly of a large band of rebels near Woodstock and in the dispatch of government forces under Lord Grey of Wilton to oppose them. The insurgents retreated into the Cotswolds and were finally attacked and dispersed in the region of Chipping Norton. Many of the rebels were slain in battle and some two hundred were taken prisoner. After his victory Grey called a meeting of the gentlemen of the shire on July 19 to arrange the execution of numbers of his captives in disaffected areas throughout the county.[3]

Some of these risings were mere local brawls, but in a period of widespread discontent what began as an outbreak of some local quarrel might easily become a major riot, as was the case at Wymondham. A number of the risings of that unsettled summer presented serious threats to life and property over considerable areas, overturning for a time local law and authority. Two of the risings, that of Kett and the rebellion in Devon, brought large bands of rebels into the field to terrorise major cities and to withstand for some weeks the heaviest forces the Protector could send against them.

Most of the risings were dealt with by the local gentry acting variously as the King's lieutenants, as local law officers, or simply as landlords protecting their interests. The methods adopted varied from county to county depending upon such factors as the local causes of popular grievance, the nature and extent of the disturbance, and the personalities of the local governors. Popular uprisings in the sixteenth century were to be handled if possible by the local nobility and agents of the Crown, and in times of emergency these authorities had the widest discretion. Methods of keeping the peace in the summer of 1549 varied from the swift capital reprisals delivered by Sir William Herbert to the Earl of Arundel's gentle request that the rebels come individually to tell him their troubles at Arundel Castle. Only when the situation was manifestly beyond the resources of the resident authorities, or when, as in Hampshire and Norfolk, there was no effective local policy, would forces be allocated by the government.

The government was reluctant to send forces into the rebellious counties. Somerset hoped almost to the last that a policy of lenience, conciliation, and gradual redress of grievances would obviate the necessity for military action. There was, moreover, a natural unwillingness in the Council to send forces out into the eastern and western extremities of the kingdom at a time when a war was being fought on the northern border, when war with France was imminent, and when the capital itself needed defence against rebellious groups in the southeast. The government had insufficient forces to meet the demands of its foreign policy, and most of the forces it had were mercenaries, German or Italian, which it was obviously inadvisable to use in quelling domestic opposition. When serious risings broke out simultaneously in widely separated parts of England it was possible to send substantial military aid only to places where there was most urgent need. Even so, there were often long delays in the arrival of promised troops, and in places the rebels were left virtually unopposed for weeks.

The rebellions in Norfolk and Devon were by far the most serious of those which occurred in 1549, and by mid-August almost all the professional armed forces in the kingdom were involved in one of these two areas. That the two longest and strongest outbreaks of violent discontent should have occurred in the eastern and western extremities of the country can be attributed partly to the respective political structures of these areas and partly to their being at some distance from London. Distance from the capital was an important factor in both risings: combined with the absence of strong local forces it gave the rebels time to assemble, recruit, and move, while the government was forced to wait for information and to dispatch forces on relatively long marches. The longevity and temporary successes of these two risings can be understood only in the light of the overall military situation in the summer of 1549, and of their simultaneous occurrence at opposite ends of the kingdom. Had the Council been able to send all its forces in one direction there can be no doubt that order would have been restored much sooner.

Because the risings in Norfolk and Devon were contemporaneous, and because each served to divert armies that would otherwise have been sent against the other, some account of the events in the west is relevant to the rebellion in the east.[4] The rising in the west began in two or three different places as spontaneous and uncoordinated actions which, achieving initial success, coalesced and progressed to greater endeavours. As long as they encountered no opposing force of real strength the rebels found that success bred success until, having added to their numbers as many sympathizers as the area would afford, they sat down outside the city of Exeter. The same pattern was followed by both rebellions: in each case once the rebel force stopped moving it virtually stopped recruiting and its eventual dissolution became inevitable. In time the government would muster sufficient strength to defeat and disperse the rebels in a pitched battle.

The primary motive behind the western rising seems to have been a conservative distaste for the religious reforms of Cranmer and Somerset, but there is no doubt that social and economic factors were also of importance. The religious colouring given to the western rebels' intentions by the lists of demands and grievances they put into writing may in part be explained by the number of priests who were prominent in the affair and who would naturally have had much to do with the composition of its documents. Relatively few priests appear to have been involved in Kett's rebellion, and the generally secular nature of Kett's written demands simply reflects the intersts of the laymen who composed them.

In the spring of 1549 a body of insurgents under the leadership of Humphry Arundell of Helland set out from Bodmin across the moors with the intention of marching on London. At about the same time another rebel force marched southwards and occupied Plymouth. An independent rising began in Devonshire in the village of Sampford Courtenay, where a gentleman named Hellier was murdered on June 9 by a mob which then took to the roads and headed for Exeter. In the region of Crediton the forces from Bodmin and Sampford Courtenay combined and established a camp.

The government set Sir Gawen Carew and his nephew Sir Peter

Carew, both men of influence in the west, to assemble the local justices and offer pardon to the rebels on condition of their dispersal. The Carews encountered strong hostility from the rebels, and when their offer of pardon met with no indication of compliance Sir Peter returned to recommend to Somerset that forces be sent to restore order. Although this report was unwelcome to the Protector and caused him, unfairly, to criticise Carew's conduct of his mission, a force was dispatched on June 24 under John, Lord Russell, the Lord Privy Seal and one of the Council appointed by the will of Henry VIII. The choice of Russell for this task was determined by his ownership of extensive lands in the southwest, monastic lands granted him by the late King, which made him, in principle, a person of some power and authority in that region. But Russell, who was not much used to military command, proved unduly cautious and slow to act, allowing more than a month to elapse before he felt sufficiently reinforced to chance a decisive engagement with the rebels. He was, however, victorious in the end, and he emerged from the siege of Exeter in command of one of the two armies at large in the country, a command which gave him a strong voice in the change of government in the autumn and which in effect won for him the earldom of Bedford conferred in the next year.

Acting on the advice of the Carews, Russell had halted in his march westward and established a base camp at Mohun's Ottery, just east of Honiton. There he stayed for some time, demanding substantial reinforcements before he would venture against the rebels. The government had few forces to spare, men being needed for the defense of the capital and for Warwick's expedition to Norfolk. The armies of Grey and Herbert were ordered to join Russell, but neither was able to do so until August. By the end of July the Council was strongly urging Russell to advance on Exeter with what forces he had, but Russell would take no action against the superior numbers of the besiegers. Fortunately Exeter held out. The strongly-worded injunctions which Russell received from Somerset no doubt did much to turn him against the Protector, in whose fate he was to have a decisive voice in October.

On July 29 Russell won a victory at Fenny Bridges some four miles west of Honiton, but he sustained considerable losses and did not prevent the rebels from regrouping in front of Exeter. For some five days Russell waited, and then, supported by Lord Grey, began his advance on August 3. After a number of engagements the rebels were forced to withdraw westwards from Exeter on August 6, when Russell camped triumphantly before the walls of the delivered city. Here Russell paused again, although a substantial rebel force was still in being, and waited ten days before moving in pursuit. In the meantime he was joined by

Herbert and so commanded the largest army in the kingdom, a force disproportionately large for the task which remained for it. A victory over the rebels was obtained at Sampford Courtenay on August 18, and Arundell, their leader, was captured at Launceston shortly afterwards. Ten days after the battle at Sampford Courtenay Kett was brought in captivity to the Earl of Warwick in Norwich, and by the end of August the great rebellions of 1549 were over.

6. *The Military Situation*

The military situation of England must have seemed grave in the early days of August, 1549. There had been war with Scotland since the end of 1543, and the French, who were increasingly aiding the Scots, made an open declaration of hostilities on August 8. English forces were therefore engaged both in the north and southwards across the Channel, where Calais and Boulogne, then English possessions, had to be garrisoned against the French. At the same time a much more immediate threat came from the eastern and western rebellions, both still strong and both draining the scant military resources of the government. Between foreign enemies and domestic dissidents England was threatened from all sides.

The war with Scotland had begun in 1543 when the Scots repudiated the treaty concluded earlier that year with the Earl of Arran (acting as Regent for the infant Queen Mary). The treaty promised the betrothal of Mary, then scarcely a year old, to Henry's son Edward, born some six years before, and was intended to secure the eventual union of the two crowns and the two countries. To enforce this treaty Henry went to war, and Somerset, who (as Earl of Hertford) was frequently commander of the armies Henry sent northwards, continued as Protector to try by force of arms to achieve this royal marriage. In spite of some spectacular military successes, however, this aggressive policy did little but arouse increasingly determined opposition from the Scots, and this in turn, as at other points in the history of the three nations, encouraged the French to aid the Scots with the object of weakening England's power of intervention in continental affairs.

Francis I of France died on March 31, 1547, and was succeeded by the more overtly anti-English Henry II, who at once began reinforcing the Scots. Substantial French armies were sent over to Scotland and, more seriously, the young Queen Mary was sent to France for safety. This was a grave blow to Somerset's policy: Mary remained in France for thirteen years, received a French education, and, in 1558, married the French prince who became Francis II. The war in Scotland continued although, after the departure of Mary, neither the French nor the English stood to gain much by its prolongation: apart from the siege of Haddington, which lasted into September, 1549, there was in fact little serious fighting in the north in the last year of the Protectorate.

The French declaration of war was prompted by the internal problems of England which, it was hoped, would incapacitate her from serious defence of her continental interests. Had it not been that the garrison towns of Calais and Boulogne were held by the English the war with France would have made little difference to the military situation: the French had already been giving the Scots as much aid as they could for the preceding two years, and the chance of a French invasion of the English mainland (as opposed to mere coastal raids, which were not unusual) was small. Calais and Boulogne, however, had to be defended. Besides their economic and political value as England's foothold on the continent must be considered the consequence of their loss to the government responsible. Calais and Boulogne represented hard-won English victories over the traditional enemy, and Somerset, in difficulties enough already, could not let these towns fall to France without an effort to save them. The French declaraction of war therefore added to the government's problems in August, 1549, in that it raised yet another demand for troops which were already in too short supply.

The French and Scottish wars, however, presented no immediately dangerous threat. The real military problem for Somerset was posed by the two large rebel forces lying at opposite ends of the country. The rebel armies around Exeter appear to have numbered between four and six thousand. Traditional estimates place Kett's force on Mousehold Heath at twenty thousand men[1] and although this is certainly too high his army must have ranged between ten and fifteen thousand, for Warwick's forces sent against Kett seems to have numbered, according to more reliable sources, about ten thousand. Altogether there would seem to have been well over twenty thousand men in organized rebellion by the end of July, a serious difficulty for a government whose forces were almost entirely employed abroad.

Rebellion arising from popular discontent (as opposed, for instance, to the rebellion of powerful nobles or of political sects or factions) presented particular problems in that it impeded the normal means whereby a force to face the rebels could be recruited. In an age when governments did not maintain standing armies in peacetime (beyond small forces to act as the royal bodyguard) the procedure in the event of need was to commission the recruitment of an army from the populace, the officers and leaders being supplied by the gentry and nobility as a matter of duty to the King; but when, as in 1549, the populace from among whom the army was to be raised was sympathetic to the rebels whom the army was to oppose the system was in danger of breaking down. In July, for example, Russell found great difficulty in adding to the small professional forces the government sent him, and he found his ranks constantly depleted by desertion. If the local gentry had been unable to organize local forces to oppose an uprising there was little hope for an outsider, no matter what his commission, sent from London to do so. With most of the country in a state of more or less strongly expressed disaffection, where were the necessary troops to be found?

Foreign mercenaries were the obvious answer, but the use of foreign forces against the already aggrieved English commons would add weight and sympathy to the rebel cause. In the summer of 1549 the government had no alternative, and mercenaries appear to have provided the core of each of the armies used to put down the rebellions.

The several armies employed for these purposes can best be distinguished by the names of their respective commanders – Warwick, Northampton, Russell, Grey, Willoughby and Herbert. Their numbers are doubtful, and probably fluctuated considerably from week to week, as, no doubt, did the numbers of the rebels. Russell's commission to pacify the west appears to have been issued on June 24. He set off from London with a small force and was expected to recruit a large army on the way westwards. About the same time Lord Grey was sent into Oxfordshire and Buckinghamshire to restore order there and then to unite with Russell. Grey was delayed by the Oxfordshire rising, and Russell, asking for immediate reinforcement, was sent, on about July 10, one hundred and fifty Italian hackbutters from London and three or four hundred cavalry from Grey's force. At this point the Council appears to have had left at its own disposal only some four hundred mercenary horse and one thousand German foot, but there was still Herbert's force in Gloucestershire, now largely unoccupied, which was ordered to be in readiness. Russell now commanded around 1,350 professional soldiers, but because Grey was still held down in Oxfordshire Russell requested further reinforcements before moving from the region of Honiton to the relief of Exeter. This time the Council could send only one hundred and sixty hackbutters, being now concerned with assembling a force for Northampton to lead against Kett. In mid July Lord Willoughby was made captain-general of Lincolnshire and Norfolk and dispatched to levy forces there for action against Kett. Willoughby appears to have made his first object the defense of King's Lynn against riotous groups in the surrounding countryside. Northampton's army, which entered Norwich on July 31, numbered perhaps 1,500, including a considerable party of Italian mercenaries. The force was far too small if contemporary estimates of Kett's numbers have any basis in fact, but Northampton did succeed, it would appear, in withdrawing most of his men safely to Cambridge, where they later joined with Warwick's much larger army.

Northampton's defeat, Russell's demands for more troops, and the imminent threat of war from France placed severe strains on the government's military resources. The situation in the west was soon eased, however, for Grey at last joined Russell in the advance on Exeter, bringing with him a force which included two hundred horse and about three hundred Italian mercenaries, and the city was shortly relieved. While Russell rested in Exeter, moreover, Herbert arrived with a force of four or five thousand, consisting mostly of footsoldiers from Wales, Gloucestershire, and Wiltshire, making the government's ultimate success in the west virtually certain. Russell seems to have commanded well over eight thousand men in the last days of his campaign.

Exeter was relieved on August 6, and four days later Warwick acknowledged receipt of his orders for the suppression of Kett. On August 21 he joined forces with Northampton at Cambridge, where Captain Drury had been waiting for some time with a band of soldiers from London. At King's Lynn close by Lord Willoughby had assembled troops recruited from Lincolnshire and Cambridgeshire, intending to march on rebel centres either at Walsingham or Hingham. Neighbouring towns were sending what levies they could to join him: the Corporation Records of Wisbech, for instance, note the dispatch of thirty-seven men. When Warwick's force entered Norfolk Willoughby abandoned his own plans and joined the Earl on the way to Norwich, which they reached on July 24. Warwick's final strength is variously estimated, Sotherton and Neville giving twelve or fourteen thousand and Edward VI, in his Journal, six thousand foot and fifteen hundred horse. On August 26 he was reinforced by 1,400 German mercenaries (lancers, or "lanzknechts") whose arrival tipped the military balance in Warwick's favour and may well have precipitated the final battle of Dussindale which was fought on the next day.

By the end of August England, officially at war with France and Scotland, had put down the serious rebellions at home and had two large forces, Russell's in the west and Warwick's in the east, whose immediate tasks were accomplished. Had the wars been pressing the obvious course would have been to direct one of these forces northwards and to hold the other in the south to guard against invasion and to reinforce Calais and Boulogne, but the foreign wars were not pressing and the two armies, whose leaders both had good reason to dislike the Protector's government, slowly turned towards London.

7. *The Situation in Norfolk*

Why did the rebellions in Norfolk and the southwest reach such grave proportions while contemporaneous risings in other areas were relatively small, brief, and confined? One explanation lies in their distance from London: the time necessary for the government to collect reliable information and put the requisite forces on the spot allowed both rebel armies to reach a substantial size and to achieve a measure of organization before they met effective opposition. If distance from the capital were the only explanation, however, there would surely have been major risings in the north and in the region of Wales. The disturbances in the northern and other remoter counties did not reach the proportions of the Norfolk and Devon risings because of the presence and prompt action there of strong local upholders of authority. The gentry in Norfolk and the southwest were without decisive leadership because, in both areas, the representatives of the great mediaeval families had recently been removed causing a breakdown in the long-established local power structures. Henry Courtenay, Earl of Devon and Marquess of Exeter, heir of the family which had held lands in the southwest since the early thirteenth century, had been attainted and executed in 1539. He had at one time enjoyed the favour of Henry VIII and had considerably extended his estates by grants of monastic lands, only to be found guilty of treasonous correspondence with the exiled Cardinal Pole. Because he was attainted his estates were forfeit to the Crown, and Henry, to replace the Courtenays in Devon with a family more dependent upon himself, granted much of this property to Russell. When trouble arose in the west Russell was therefore deputed to deal with it, but he had not had time to acquire anything like the local influence of the vanished Courtenays.

Much the same had happened in Norfolk where the Howards, heirs of the Bigods and the Mowbrays, had been the greatest landlords in East Anglia ever since the reign of Edward IV.[1] Thomas Howard, third Duke of Norfolk, had been attainted and sent to the Tower in 1546 for complicity in the treason of his son Henry, styled Earl of Surrey, who was executed in January, 1547. The estates of both father and son were forfeit to the Crown, but the father, saved from execution by the accident of Henry's death, remained to be restored to lands and titles on the accession of Queen Mary. Throughout the six-year reign of Edward VI Thomas Howard was a prisoner and there was no Duke of Norfolk. When trouble arose in East Anglia there was no local power to oppose it.

The attainders of the Howards and of the Marquess of Exeter are instances of Henry's desire, especially in his later years when the problem of the succession loomed large, to eliminate the few surviving baronial powers in the realm which might command sufficient strength and prestige to challenge the Crown. (By the time of Henry's death about half the peerage owed their titles and lands to the Tudor dynasty.) The Howards and the Courtenays were suspect to Henry not only as powerful heirs of the old nobility but also as dangerously close in blood to the Plantagenet kings whom the Tudors had supplanted in 1485. They were potential claimants of the throne itself, and their titles, on paper at least, were as strong as Henry's own. Both Henry Courtenay and Henry Howard were grandsons of Edward IV, and Henry Tudor, if we disregard the battle of Bosworth, was no more.

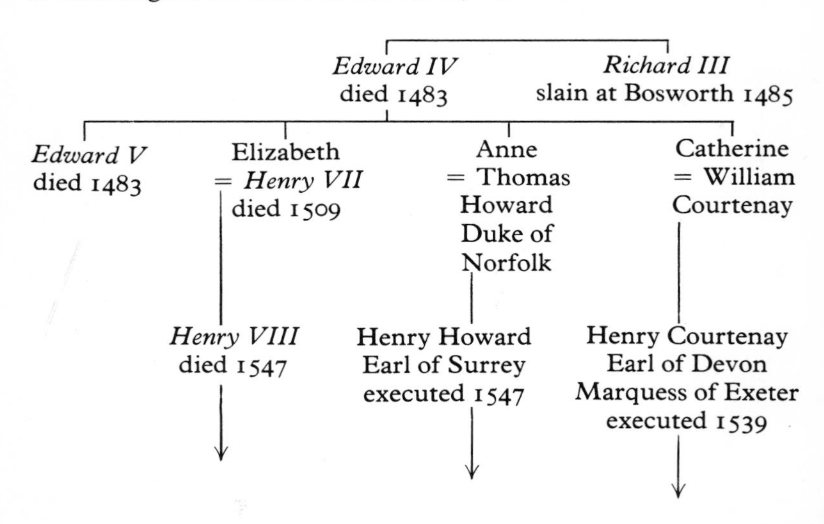

Henry's reasons for wishing the removal of the Howards and the Courtenays are to be found in this genealogy rather than in the charges brought at the trials. Ironically it is probably true in both cases that Henry's excessive desire to remove all rivals to the throne contributed, by upsetting the patterns of local authority, to the causes of the rebellions in Devon and in Norfolk in 1549.

The details of Courtenay's trial do not concern us, but Surrey's treason is a Norfolk matter. The chief point in the accusation against Surrey was that he had caused to be displayed in the Howard mansion at Kenninghall a quartering of the arms of Edward the Confessor with those of Howard, which act, it was alleged, constituted treason, for only the King might bear the arms of the Confessor. That Surrey did display such a coat of arms is not certain, neither is it clear that for him to have done so would have been criminal, but these difficulties were only superficial. The real reasons for the fall of the Howards lay not so much in any act of theirs as in the political aims of the Seymours and of the King. The Seymours were opposed to the Howards not only as reformists in religion but also in more personal ways. The Howards were at the head of the old, pre-Tudor, nobility, and tended to look down on newly risen families such as the Russells, Dudleys, and Seymours. Strong rivalry and open enmity developed between Hertford and Surrey, and on at least one occasion resulted in bodily assault. The balance was finally tipped in favour of the Seymours against the Howards by the fact that Henry's two marriages with members of the Norfolk family[2] had ended in bitterness and the block, whereas his Seymour wife had given him his only surviving son.

The chief accuser of Surrey was Sir Richard Southwell of Woodrising, a distant cousin of the Howards who had received his upbringing in their household as a companion of the Earl. Because the alleged offence had been committed in Norfolk the case was sent to Norwich for trial before a jury of Norfolk gentlemen: its members were Sir William Paston, Sir James Boleyn, Sir Francis Lovell, Sir Richard Gresham,[3] Sir John Clere, Thomas Clere, William Wodehouse, Christopher Heydon, Nicholas Le Strange, Philip Hubbert, and Henry Bedingfield. The trial was held in Norwich Guildhall on January 13, 1547, and eight days later Surrey was beheaded on Tower Hill. He left two sons, the elder of whom succeeded as fourth Duke of Norfolk in 1554 and was himself attainted and executed in 1572.

The eclipse of the Howards left no family of great nobility or national importance among the governors and landowners of Norfolk. There were several families of local prominence whose names were already known to court and Parliament and whose members were to achieve nobility and high office in the future – the Townshends of Raynham, the Wodehouses of Kimberley, the Pastons of Caister and Oxnead, and the Wyndhams of Felbrigg – and some of these, like the Le Stranges of Hunstanton and the Bedingfields of Oxborough, were of much greater antiquity than the Howards. But no one of these families in 1549 was so great in Norfolk as to be able to give leadership to the rest.[4] The dozen or so prominent families of the county appear to have been left in a general state of mutual rivalry after the fall of the Howards, each hoping to outdo the others in a scramble for lands, offices, and royal favour. Although most of the gentry within the vicinity of Norwich appear to have contributed some resistance to Kett they achieved no concerted action for some time. The leaderless, factious state of the Norfolk gentry gave Kett the chance to build his army and establish a strong position before effective opposition could be brought against him.

The situation may have been aggravated by the weakness in 1549 of another centre of authority in the county, the bishopric of Norwich, at that time held by the unpopular William Rugge. In the thirteen years since his election Rugge, Abbot of St. Bennet of Holme, had brought the see of Norwich to the brink of financial ruin and acquired a reputation for cruel and reactionary policies. In the year of the rising a petition was sent from Norfolk to the King complaining of the Bishop's conduct, as a result of which Rugge was compelled to resign on a moderate pension. Rugge had a brother Robert who was a sheriff of Norwich in 1537 and mayor in 1545 and 1550, which suggests that the Bishop might once have had some influence on the affairs of the city, but by the time of the rising his days were evidently numbered. Even if Rugge remained in Norwich until the appointment of his successor, Thomas Thirlby, in April, 1550, he played no part in the city's resistance to Kett's army.

Kett's rebellion in Norfolk achieved the proportions it did because of the unusual conditions prevalent in the county in 1549 which allowed the insurgents to congregate and march on Norwich without effective opposition. The rising began in Wymondham where the feast of St. Thomas of Canterbury brought together a sizeable crowd of people, provided an opportunity for the discussion of grievances, and added to the sum of popular discontents the local dissatisfaction with the conduct of the dissolution of the Abbey. The congregation of people, the presence of Kett, and the local dislike of Flowerdew combined to give impetus to what might otherwise have ended as a holiday brawl. Such disturbances over enclosures and in pursuit of local feuds had been frequent in Norfolk in previous years, but until Kett and his followers took the Norwich road all had been ended quickly by recourse to law, by the prompt action of the authorities, or by simple inertia.

In 1520 there had been disturbances in Fakenham where Sir Henry Fermor was said to have laid down extensive sheep walks to the detriment of the commons. In 1539 there were riots at Hingham against the enclosures of Sir Henry Parker. At Griston in the next year one John Walker attempted to organize popular discontent into an armed rising against the gentry. In 1544 there

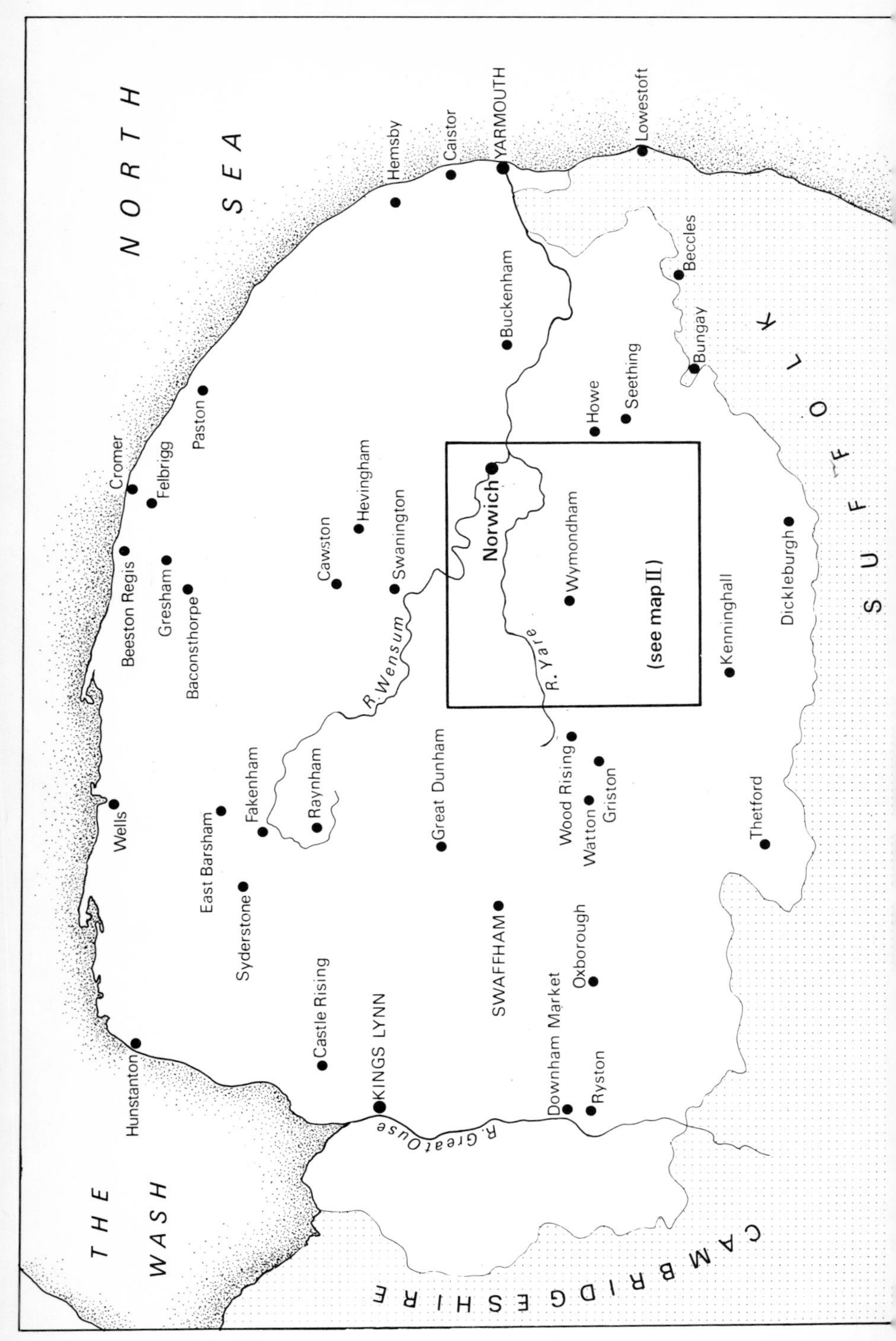

Map I. Norfolk, showing places mentioned in the text

were riots against enclosures in Great Dunham. Early in the reign of Edward VI a band of commoners gathered at Castle Rising threatening the nearby town of King's Lynn and were with some difficulty dispersed by a company of gentry. In the years immediately before Kett's rising there were disputes about enclosures at Middleton, a case which came before the Court of Star Chamber in the summer of 1549. Each of these disturbances was contained: the gentry made a show of strength, a legal redress was sought, or the rioters, having made their demonstration, dispersed of their own accord because they had no leader and no long-term plans. At Wymondham a number of causes and a large number of people came fortuitously together with a capable leader who seems to have given them a revolutionary purpose.

John Green, lord of the manor of Wilby, had enclosed common lands in the neighbouring villages of Hargham and Attleborough. On the night of June 20 the inhabitants of Attleborough, Eccles, and Wilby had thrown down Green's fences and returned to their houses before morning. The suddenness and single-mindedness with which people from several villages separated by as much as five miles operated that night suggests a degree of planning and organization. Attleborough, the largest of these communities, is less than six miles southwest of Wymondham and there can be little doubt that John Green's broken fences were a subject of lively conversation at the festival of St. Thomas only seventeen days later. The roots of the rising are only partly in Wymondham itself: the first disturbances which seem to be connected with what was to become Kett's rebellion occurred in a group of villages to the south and west of the Abbey town. In the southwest quarter of a circle of eleven mile radius drawn around Wymondham lie not only Attleborough, Wilby, Eccles, and Hargham, but also Griston and Hingham. Also in this sector are the villages of Morley St. Botolph and Morley St. Peter, which were the first objective of the Wymondham rebels on July 8. The fences of Mr. Hobart at Morley, about three miles from the town, were thrown down before the men from Wymondham turned to Flowerdew's properties in Hethersett.

Disturbances contemporary with Kett's occurred elsewhere in Norfolk, in Castle Rising, for instance, and there were others across the border in Suffolk, involving Bungay and Beccles. Nowhere else in East Anglia, however, was there such a concentration of disorders as in this region to the southwest of Wymondham. The feast of St. Thomas brought the inhabitants of these villages together, and in the activities of the following Monday (July 8) we begin to see the fruits of their consultations. Two local landlords, Hobart and Flowerdew, were attacked in quick succession. The third was Robert Kett.

8. *The March on Norwich*

Sunday July 7, 1549, saw the celebration of the feast of St. Thomas at Wymondham, the festivities including the traditional church play. On the following day, almost certainly as a result of conversations held the day before, a small band of men set off from Wymondham, walked some three miles southwestwards, and demolished the offending fences at Morley. They then turned back and went some six miles in the opposite direction, presumably returning through the town, and attacked the fences of Sir John Flowerdew at Hethersett.

Flowerdew was a professional man, a lawyer, in the process of raising his family into the ranks of the gentry. His efforts in this pursuit, his enclosures and his service as the King's agent in the disposal of the Abbey property, inevitably aroused local hostility. Lawyers rarely enjoy popularity, and Flowerdew appears to have been a reasonably successful lawyer. He was a Sergeant at Law, evidently trusted by the crown, and his son Edward, another lawyer, was to become a Baron of the Exchequer in the reign of Elizabeth. The importance of Flowerdew's unpopularity in the origins of the rebellion should not, however, be overestimated: had hatred of the Sergeant been a decisive factor the crowd would surely have attacked him first and would certainly not then have allowed Flowerdew to persuade them to leave him in peace.

Flowerdew in person confronted the rioters on the way to Hethersett and suggested they turn their attention to the enclosures of Robert Kett in Wymondham. The suggestion was backed by a sum of money, a bribe, said to have been forty pence. For this to be a meaningful sum the crowd must still have been quite small, perhaps as few as a dozen. They accepted Flowerdew's advice and his money, and retraced their steps once more. Their willingness to be turned, first by Flowerdew to Kett and later by Kett back to Flowerdew, shows that they had as yet no definite plan or long range intention. Had Flowerdew not directed them to Kett they might, like their neighbours in Attleborough and Wilby, have simply thrown down the fences and gone back to their homes.

The great and insoluble mystery of the affair is why Kett, who like Flowerdew represented a rising local landowning family, should have turned his back on home and fortune to lead a popular rebellion. His taking the rebels back to Hethersett was a fair reprisal against Flowerdew, but it is impossible now to guess the motives which prompted him next day to put himself at their head in a march on Norwich.

In 1549 Robert Kett was some fifty-seven years old and a man of extensive property in the Wymondham area. He was married, probably to Alice Appleyard, daughter of another local landowner, and was father of four, or perhaps five, sons. He was himself the fourth of the five sons of Thomas Kett of Forncett who had died in 1536. Two, and possibly three, of his brothers were dead by 1549, but William, the eldest, was living. William Kett, Robert's senior by some seven years, is described as a "butcher" – which means a grazier rather than a purveyor of meat – and as a mercer. He may well have owned a mercer's shop in Wymondham, but he was, no less than his brother, primarily a wealthy gentleman farmer. He may in fact have been the wealthier of the two, for he was the elder and had inherited the portion of at least one of their deceased brothers.[1]

When Robert Kett heard that rioters were, at the Sergeant's instigation, attacking his enclosures he joined them, agreeing that his own fences should be removed, and took them back to Hethersett to complete the work they had left there. The turning point came some time in the next eighteen hours when it was decided that the crowd should reassemble on the next day (Tuesday) and proceed to Norwich. The decision may be presumed to have been taken largely by Kett, for until he joined the rioters they obviously had no such plan. It was Kett who turned the rising from a local squabble between villagers and landowners into a matter of national concern.

By the morning of Tuesday, July 9, it had been decided that the riot was not to end with its work of the previous day, nor was its work for the future to be confined to the immediate vicinity of Wymondham. Kett had agreed to lead the protesting commons in a march on Norwich, which inevitably meant an attempt to influence not only the local landowners but also the national government. And William Kett had in the meantime decided to join them. The party which set out for Norwich was of substantial size. The numbers involved in the action of the Monday were probably small, as is suggested by the manageability of the crowd and its amenability to a bribe of forty pence, but the rioters of the next day were of sufficient numbers to alarm the Norwich city authorities into sending, on that same day, appeals for aid to the local gentry and even to the King at Windsor.

From Wymondham to Norwich is only some nine miles: by the end of the day Kett's force was within two miles of the city and beginning to circle northwards around it. His intentions, whether or not they were announced to the citizens, must have been obvious. There would be no point in by-passing Norwich to continue northwards or eastwards, where nothing lies but villages, small ports, and the sea: his army was unmistakably aimed at the city itself. By the end of the day the city council had dispatched messengers requesting help to the King, to Sir Roger Townshend, and to Sir William Paston.

The Townshends and the Pastons had both made their family fortunes through the practise of law and through marriages with local heiresses. At this time the Pastons, having enjoyed several generations of royal favour and holding extensive property mostly in east Norfolk, were the greater family of the two. Sir Roger Townshend's seat was at Raynham, twenty-five miles west of Norwich, Sir William Paston's at Caister, some twenty miles east. It is not recorded that Townshend made any response to the city's appeal. Sir William Paston, however, sent two large cannon, which were to be of some service until captured by the rebels. Sir William, an eminent lawyer whose name heads the list of jurors at Surrey's trial, was at this time around seventy years of age and could perhaps have done no more. He died five years later.

The city appealed to Paston and Townshend as prominent local gentry whose influence might conceivably have been sufficient to mount some kind of effective opposition to the rebels. An adequate show of strength might have dispersed them at this early stage, but there was scarcely time to have organized such a force before Kett reached Mousehold. The collection of a force would have required the concerted action of the gentry, but the chief of these, like Paston and Townshend were often fifty miles apart and seem to have been caught wholly unprepared by events.

Kett's force marched seven miles towards Norwich, passing through Hethersett and Cringleford. The first three miles out of Wymondham covered the same ground that some of the party had trodden twice the day before in the two excursions to Sergeant Flowerdew's fences. According to tradition an oath was sworn near Hethersett at the point on the road marked by "Kett's Oak". The tree, which is carefully preserved by the county council, may have been a predetermined meeting point for those wishing to join the march. It should not be confused with the vanished "Oak of Reformation" which stood on Mousehold Heath, or with another "Kett's Oak" at Ryston which, according to Russell, marks the spot where a band of the rebels from Castle Rising camped on their way to join the men on Mousehold. Kett's association with oak trees is part of the legend which has grown up around this enigmatic figure. Some writers, in defiance of incontrovertible sources, have even had Kett hanged from one of his oaks.[2]

At Cringleford the crowd crossed the river Yare. They were

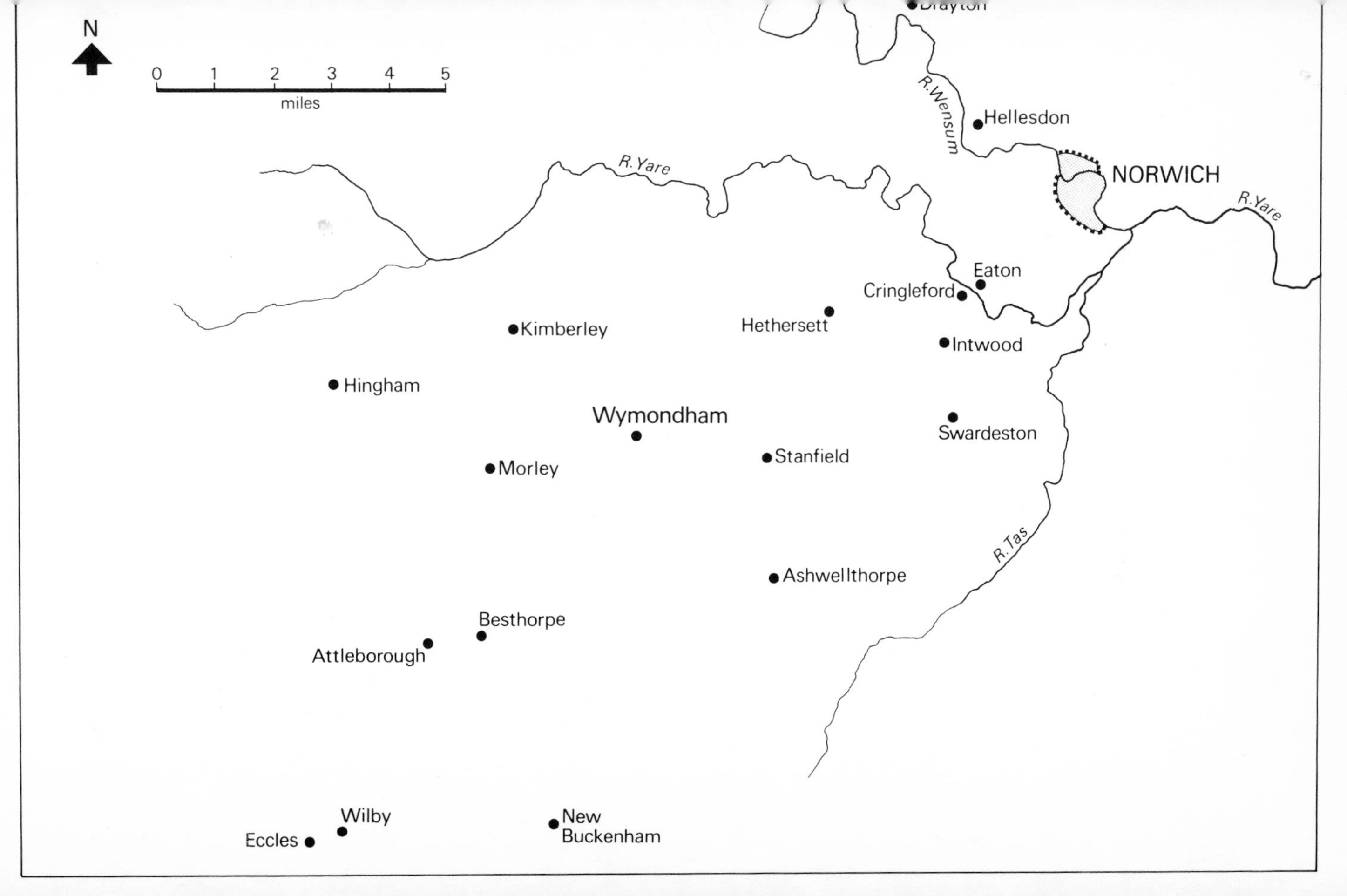

Map II. Wymondham and surrounding villages

then within two miles of the city walls, but instead of continuing their direct approach they turned northwards and began skirting the west side of the city at a considerable distance. Perhaps Kett had already received notice that the city would resist him, or perhaps he wished to take time to rest his men and increase their numbers before beginning negotiations with the city council. The first camp was made at Bowthorpe, about two miles westwards from the city. Here the rioters took the opportunity to pull down the fences of the town close, an area enclosed by the city. Any citizen, on payment of one halfpenny per week per beast, could graze his animals in the close. The arrangement, which included the employment of a herdsman to oversee the area, seems to have been in the general interest, but the fences and the fees evidently aroused resentment. Kett's men appear to have been joined in this undertaking by some people from Norwich: according to some sources the townspeople threw down the close fences themselves even before the men from Wymondham arrived. There is no doubt that Kett did receive considerable support from the poorer people in the city, many of whom joined him at Bowthorpe or later on Mousehold while others remained in the city to help with diversionary riots when fighting broke out between the city and the camp.

While Kett was camped at Bowthorpe, either on the evening of July 9 or the morning of July 10, the rioters were approached by Sir Edmund Wyndham of Felbrigg, High Sheriff of Norfolk and Suffolk, who proclaimed them rebels and commanded them in the King's name to disperse. Wyndham, having been informed by virtue of his office of the disturbances at Wymondham,[3] had come to restore order. In the absence of the Lord Lieutenant (formerly the Duke of Norfolk and now the Marquess of Northampton) the Sheriff was the highest officer of the crown in the county. Wyndham may have ridden twenty miles from his seat at Felbrigg near Cromer, or he may have been already at hand in his official residence, Norwich Castle, but he had not had time to organize any force to oppose the rebels.

Even apart from his office of Sheriff Wyndham was perhaps the most likely of the Norfolk gentry to have led local opposition to Kett. He seems to have been a rather younger man than Sir William Paston, for he lived until 1569, and he had close family ties with the highest nobility. His grandmother had been a Howard, a daughter of the first Duke of Norfolk, and through his father's second marriage he was cousin (but not in blood) to the Lord Protector. His father had enjoyed the favour of Henry VIII and had been rewarded with the reversal of the attainder of Sir Edmund's grandfather, executed for treason in 1502. His half-brother Thomas was a successful soldier who had served with

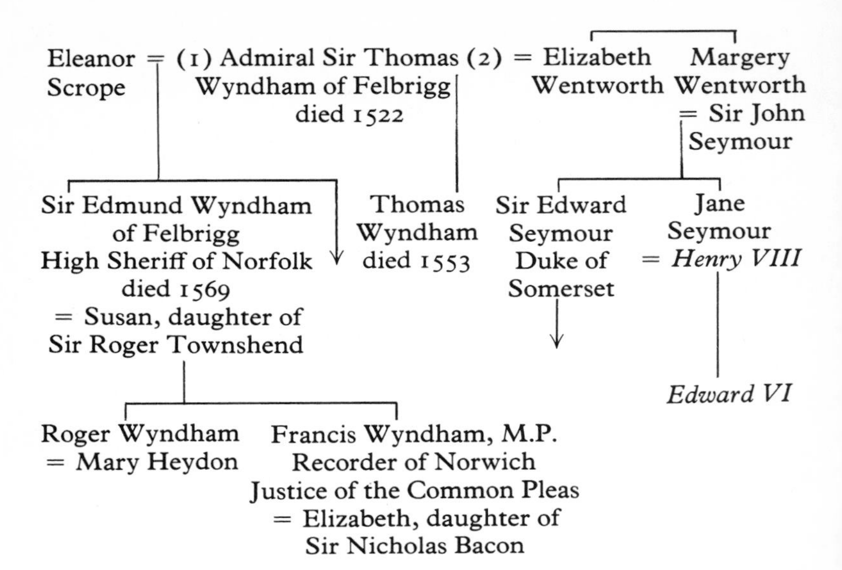

distinction as a naval commander in the recent Scottish wars. His son Francis was to marry a sister of the great Lord Bacon and to become a judge in 1592. The Wyndhams had resided at Felbrigg for almost a century and were allied by marriage to several of the Norfolk gentry, including the Townshends and the Heydons. Sir Edmund, through his father's alliance with the Seymours, had been knighted on the marriage of Queen Jane and had obtained monastic lands on the dissolution.[4]

Sir Edmund's appeal to Kett's army was rejected and Wyndham himself forced by hostile demonstrations to retreat into Norwich. What further action, if any, the Sheriff took against the rebels is not known, for his name does not reappear in the story until after Kett's trial.

Towards the evening of July 9 the camp at Bowthorpe was visited by the Mayor and principal citizens of Norwich who, like Wyndham, attempted to persuade the mob to disband. The Mayor at this time was Thomas Codd, a respectable, charitable man, and an efficient officer of local government unfortunate in that his mayoral year coincided with a situation he could not possibly have controlled. His initial policy of passive but firm resistance was no doubt the right one under the circumstances, and Codd's moderation during the first weeks of the rebellion may well have saved the city much bloodshed. That the citizens were satisfied with his conduct of affairs is suggested by the fact that he was chosen mayor again six years later in 1555. Codd was a benefactor of the church and of the poor and lies buried in the nave of St. Peter Parmentergate in Norwich.

Codd, like Wyndham, was unable to influence Kett's army. On Wednesday, July 10, it moved slightly southwards to Eaton wood, which change of direction suggests that Kett had not yet decided to make for Mousehold. The details are uncertain, but it seems likely that the army camped in Eaton wood on the Wednesday night and began moving northwards again on the following day. The decision to settle on Mousehold Heath was probably taken on Wednesday while the army was at Eaton. Once his mind had been made up Kett sent to the city council for permission to bring his men through Norwich to reach the Heath which lay on the other side of the city. The council refused, feeling that to admit such a force could not be safe and would, moreover, open them to charges of collaboration with the rebels. Kett therefore began, probably on the Thursday, the march around the north of Norwich to Mousehold Heath.

On Thursday, July 11, Kett's force crossed the Wensum at Hellesdon and camped for the night near Drayton. In the region of Hellesdon they were confronted by Sir Roger Wodehouse of Kimberley accompanied by a number of servants with two carts of beer and a third cart full of provisions. Sir Roger, whose seat at Kimberley was only three miles from Wymondham, must have been well known to the Ketts and many of their followers. He appears to have relied on an appeal to local good-fellowship, backed by his three carts of food and drink, to disperse the crowd: but he had seriously misjudged their temper. Kett commandeered the carts and his men chased and captured Sir Roger who, in putting up a fight for his liberty, was stripped of his clothing and driven into a ditch near Hellesdon bridge. Only the efforts of his servant Edgerley saved him from serious injury. Sir Roger Wodehouse, representative of a family already prominent in Norfolk for one hundred and fifty years, was held in captivity by the rebels until their final defeat at Dussindale.

The next day Kett moved eastwards around the north of the city to Sprowston where he turned southwards and so came to Mousehold Heath which overlooks Norwich from the east. At Sprowston the crowd destroyed the dovecote of John Corbet, a Norwich lawyer, which was offensive to the farmers because doves kept by the gentry would frequently despoil the poor man's crops. The dovecote of John Corbet had, until two years before, been the chapel of St. Mary Magdalen, part of the Magdalen Hospital or Lazar House founded by Herbert de Losinga, the first Bishop of Norwich, in 1196. In 1547 the lands of the hospital had been granted to Sir Robert Southwell (brother to Sir Richard, the accuser of Surrey) and to John Corbet. The chapel was destroyed by Kett: the hospital building survives today as a public library.

Kett established his headquarters on Mousehold in the mansion, known as Surrey House or St. Leonard's, on the hill called Mount Surrey or St. Leonard's Hill. The confusion of names reflected the recent history of the place which, until the dissolution, had been occupied by the Benedictine Priory of St. Leonard which was granted in 1538 to the Duke of Norfolk. When the Duke's son, the Earl of Surrey, emerged from one of his several stays in King Henry's prisons in the summer of 1543 he went into East Anglia looking for a place to live. His father's house at Kenninghall did not suit him because the Duke's mistress, Bess Holland, resided there. The Howard mansion in Norwich was at that time in too poor a condition for comfort. Surrey therefore requested and obtained from his father the property of St. Leonard's and built there the house which gave the name Mount Surrey to the site of the former Priory. This magnificent building, of which only the slightest traces remain, was occupied by Kett and used primarily as a place of confinement for his prisoners. It has been said that Kett's men destroyed Mount Surrey before they left the Heath, but this may not be so, for the Howard heir, the Earl of Arundel, appears to have entertained Queen Elizabeth there in 1578, which he could not have done if the building were ruinous.[5] At the time of Kett's occupation St. Leonard's was Crown property, having been forfeit under the attainders of Norfolk and Surrey in 1547.

Kett already had several prisoners. Even at this early stage it appears to have been the policy of the rebels to capture and hold as many of the local gentry as they could, and although quite a number of these may have made their escape with Northampton's retreating army Kett retained a sufficient number of prisoners to use them as a shield for his front ranks at the battle of Dussindale. The names of only a few of these men have been recorded. Of one, Sir Roger Wodehouse, we know already. Blomefield suggests that by the time of the arrival at Mousehold, or soon afterwards, Kett also held Sergeant Gawdy, Sergeant Catlyn, and two brothers named Appleyard.[6] Sergeant Gawdy was probably Thomas Gawdy who was Recorder of King's Lynn and Member of Parliament for Lynn in 1547, Member for Norwich in 1553, and appointed Recorder of Norwich in 1563. He died in 1566, the same year as his colleague Richard Catlyn, another lawyer, who sat with Gawdy for Norwich in the Parliament of 1553 and appears to have shared a prison with him in 1549.[7] The brothers Appleyard were the two sons, John and Philip, of Roger Appleyard of Stanfield Hall who had died some twenty years before. Stanfield is only two miles from Wymondham, and it was there that Sergeant Flowerdew had resided during his depredation of Wymondham Abbey. The

Appleyards were closely connected with Flowerdew, for their sister Frances had married his eldest son William, and perhaps for this reason the brothers were taken prisoner, perhaps on the very day that the rebels set out from Wymondham. They were not held captive for too long, for they took part in the defence of Norwich on July 21, although they may have been confined again when Kett took the city. The elder brother, John, inherited the family estates on the death of his mother in this same year, and embarked on a career somewhat complicated by the marriage, in the next year, of his half-sister Amy Robsart to Sir Robert Dudley.[8]

The collection of these prisoners in the early days of the rebellion indicates several things. First it shows that, whatever the stated aims of the rebels (in the twenty-nine "demands," for example) and whatever causes the rebellion may be discovered to have had, the rising manifested itself primarily as a war between peasant farmers and small tradesmen on the one hand and landowners, lawyers, and merchants on the other, a war between classes. Secondly, the fact that Kett had prisoners to put in Surrey House as soon as he reached Mousehold shows that the rebellion was committed to pursuit of a class war from its very first days. Thirdly, however, the fact that Kett took and held prisoners at all, when the easier course was simply to kill or rob them, shows that the rebellion had a high degree of organization and even of policy. Kett's prisoners were to serve as hostages, which indicates the rebels' willingness to bargain, and their aim to reform, not simply to smash, the social order. In this and many other ways the army on Mousehold maintained a high level of discipline and, until the end, a unified purpose. It must be emphasized that, although there was much feeling against the gentry, not one of those captured is known to have been killed or wantonly maltreated, except in the course of general battles. In this conduct there appears a degree of humanity against which the reprisals exacted by Warwick and the government, although not unusual for the times, seem viciously cruel by contrast.

9. *The Norwich Defences*

While Kett was taking his army from Wymondham to Mousehold the Norwich city council were trying to decide on a course of action. It must have been obvious to them from the first that Kett would not be content indefinitely to march and camp outside the city walls: eventually he would make demands and take no refusal. Inevitably the army would need provisions, accommodation, entertainment, and other facilities abundant in the city but scarce on the heath, and Kett's leadership would depend upon his securing them. The council had to decide on the point beyond which they would not compromise, the point at which they would commence armed resistance. Several alternatives were theoretically open to them, ranging from surrender to aggression, but any extreme course was ruled out by circumstances. To surrender to Kett, or even to admit any large part of his force into Norwich, would place the citizens in immediate danger of person and property and would probably involve them in charges of complicity with the rebels. On the other hand, an attack on Kett was beyond the council's means, especially as there was within the city widespread disaffection and sympathy for the rebels. Besides, as was wisely pointed out at a council meeting, to raise an armed force, even against rebels, without a royal warrant was technically illegal.

Judging by their subsequent conduct the council appears to have decided that the army should not be admitted into the city but that every effort to maintain good relations with the camp should be made. Accordingly, whether by explicit agreement or tacit understanding, the camp remained on Mousehold but Kett's men seem to have come and gone freely in the city while many citizens, including the Mayor and aldermen, frequently visited the camp. The situation was no doubt delicate: the city authorities could not in any official sense recognize Kett, but in order to stave off open hostilities they had, unofficially, to meet with him and allow him many concessions. Presumably this peaceful state of affairs was preserved as long as it was – that is until Kett attacked the city on July 21 ffl because each side avoided forcing the other to clarify its position. Only when such clarification was made necessary by the arrival of the King's messenger was a confrontation precipitated. As long as the situation was left in their hands Kett and Codd between them maintained a diplomatic truce.

The city was, nonetheless, strongly blamed for its conduct in the face of the rebellion. The councillors were obliged to make excuses to Northampton and Warwick, the successive lieutenants sent to disperse the rebels, and were granted pardons as if they had themselves been offenders. The strongest condemnation came from Sir John Cheke in his pamphlet *The Hurt of Sedition: How Grievous it is to a Commonwealth* published later in the year of the rebellions.

> Herein hath notably appeared what cities have faithfully served and suffered extreme danger not only of goods, but also of famine and death, rather than suffer the King's enemies to enter, and what white livered cities have not only not withstood them, but also with shame favoured them, and with mischief aided them. And I would I might praise herein all cities alike! which I would do if all were like worthy. How much and how worthily may Exeter be commended, which being in the midst of rebels unvitteled, unfurnished, unprepared, for so long a seige, did nobly hold out the continual and dangerous assault of the rebels? &c. whose example if Norwich had followed, and had not rather given place to traitor Kett, than to keep their duty, and had not sought more safeguard than honesty, and private hope more than common quietness, they had ended the rebellion sooner, and escaped themselves better, and saved the loss of the worthy Lord Sheffield, in whom was more true service for his life, than in them for their goods; and although this cannot be spoken against, a certain honest sort that were amongst them, whose praise was the greater because they were so few, yet the greater number was such that they not only obeyed the rebel for fear, but also followed him for love, and did so traitorously order the King's band under my Lord Marquess [of Northampton], that they suffered more damage out of their houses by the townsmen, than they did abroad by the rebels, whose fault as the King's majesty may pardon, so I would either the example forgotten, that no city might hereafter follow the like, or the deed be so abhorred, that others hereafter would avoid the like shame, and learn to be noble by Exeter, whose truth doth not only deserve great praises, but also great reward.[1]

But the situation at Norwich was very different from that at Exeter, and, as Blomefield observes, Cheke "knew little of the matter but by hearsay only."

The citizens had three sources of comfort: the castle, the city defences, and the fact that, due reports having been made, help would eventually come from London. The first two of these were frail and temporary resources and only in the third could firm hope be placed. The castle, which had always belonged to the crown and not to the city, had been built and situated rather to keep the citizens in order than to protect them from attack.[2] The first castle had been erected on the site, a mound partly natural and partly artificial in the centre of Norwich, by the Normans very soon after the Conquest. The Kings at first appointed constables to maintain and garrison the fortress and by the sixteenth century the High Sheriff, as the local representative of the Crown, had his official residence there. By this time, however, there are indications that the castle was falling into disuse and decay. As early as 1371 the Sheriff had complained to Edward III that the castle was in poor condition because the local people used its walls as a quarry for building stone. In the reign of Henry VII there were complaints that the earthworks surrounding the keep were being gradually levelled as the townsfolk deposited their rubbish in the ditches. In 1609 the castle was officially declared decayed, and when Cromwell needed it a little later he had to have it refortified. The castle in 1549 would therefore seem to have offered little protection. Its main use, since mediaeval times, had been as a county jail, which it remained until 1887, and as such it was used by Kett when he took the city. There is no suggestion that the castle offered any resistance to the rebels once the city had been occupied. A second use of the castle was as a vantage point from which to fire the city's artillery, but although the castle mound stands high and has an uninterrupted prospect north-eastwards to Mousehold across the valley of the Wensum the situation of the castle in the centre of Norwich meant that guns on the mound could do no significant damage beyond the city walls, the distance being too great.

The walls were more encouraging. Norwich had over two miles of defensive walls, first built in the twelfth century and systematically repaired early in the fourteenth. They covered almost two thirds of the city perimeter, the remainder, a short stretch in the northwest and a longer section in the southeast, being bounded by the river Wensum, so that the walls and the river together completely encircled the city. The walls were about twenty feet high, had circular and semi-circular towers at regular intervals, and included a dozen fortified gates. These defences appear to have been in reasonable condition in 1549 and were manned to some effect at several stages in the struggle. They were not, however, an adequate defence against Kett. In the first place, greater forces than the city could command were required to man such an extensive perimeter: it was not until Warwick's army of several thousand had entered the city that the defenders were able to hold the walls against sustained attack. Secondly, the walls did not cover the east side of the city which faced Mousehold and which bore

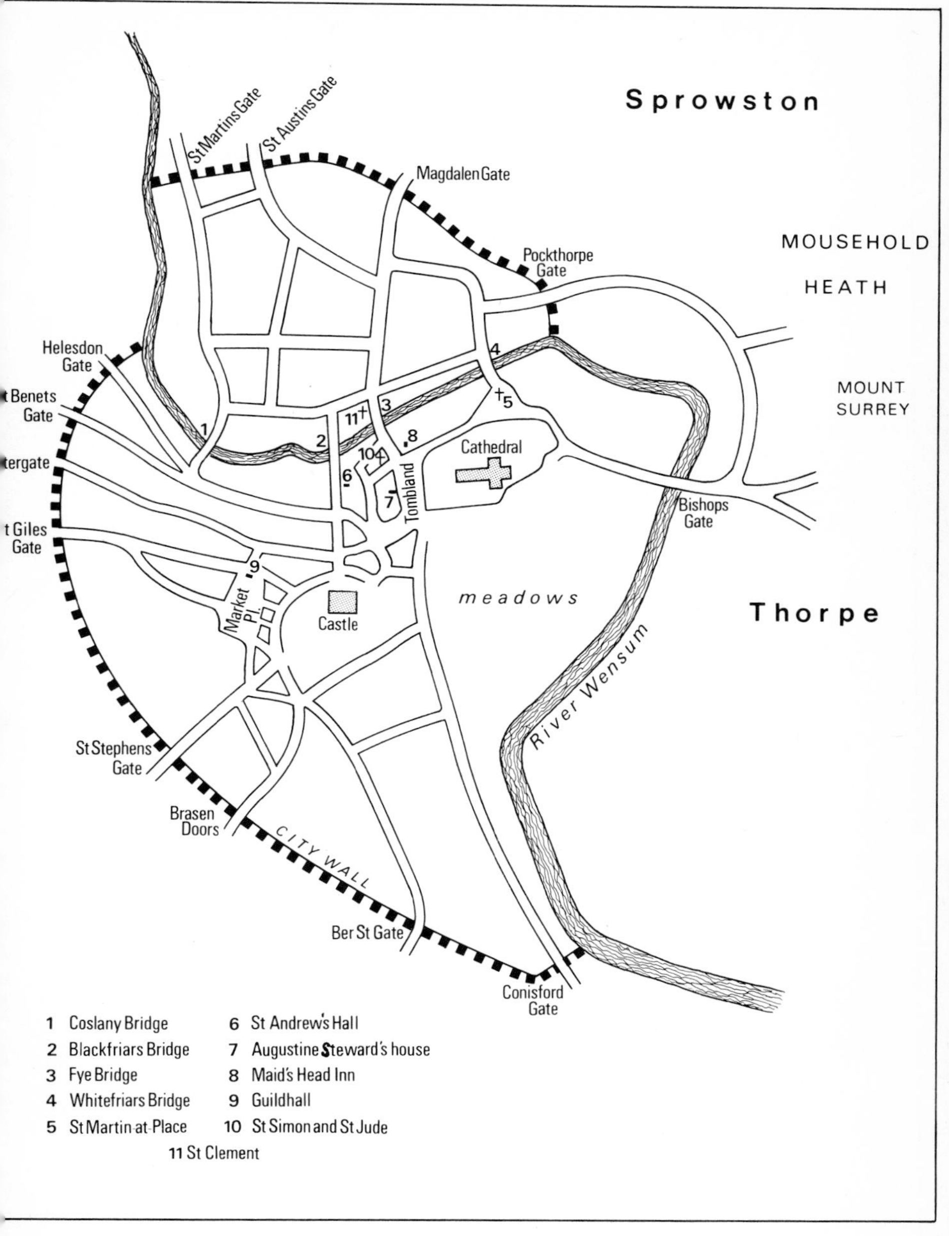

Map III. Norwich in the sixteenth century

the brunt of the rebel assault. This side was protected only by the river, which was reasonably deep and wide but which was flanked only by open meadows on both sides. Once the attackers had superior fire power they could easily clear the defenders away from the river and cover the crossing of their own men, as Kett's army appears to have done on more than one occasion. The river is, moreover, crossed on this side by the Bishopsgate bridge which, although duly fortified, was difficult to defend because of its weak and exposed position. This bridge, which is still standing, was almost opposite Mount Surrey and was the chief route by which men came and went between camp and city.

The city's weaknesses were not all in its material defences. The second city of England, with a population of over 13,000, Norwich was seriously affected by the economic problems of the mid sixteenth century. The cloth trade was declining and there appears to have been widespread unemployment even among skilled craftsmen. In May of 1549 it was reported that masons, carpenters, reeders, and tilers were leaving the city to find work. A high proportion of the city population appears to have been very poor: the assessment of 1525 revealed about thirty-five percent unable to pay the minimum rate of fourpence, and with the inflation of the intervening decades the poor had probably increased in number and found their lot becoming progressively harder. The city governors, however, came almost exclusively from the small class of wealthy merchants and landowners who controlled most of the trade and property: the figures of 1525 suggest that about six per cent of the population owned approximately sixty per cent of the city's land and wealth. Under these circumstances the council can hardly have hoped to defend their several miles of wall and river against a hostile army whose number may already have been considerably greater than that of all adult males in the city. In the event of a conflict with Kett they had as much to fear from within the walls as from without. Their only hope lay in avoiding conflict until help could arrive from London.

The castle and perimeter defences, as events were to prove, offered no security. The citizens' hope lay in the messages dispatched to London, and it was no doubt with this hope in mind that the council adopted a passively defensive policy designed to avoid serious conflict with Kett until government agents should arrive. The order of events is a little uncertain, but we know that a messenger, Edmund Pynchyn, had been sent from Norwich to the King's Council at Windsor late on July 9. If Sir Edmund Wyndham made his unsuccessful appearance before the rebels on that same day Pynchyn may well have been sent on Wyndham's instructions carrying the Sheriff's official report. At any rate, the city council could be sure that the government was informed of their plight, for with Wyndham's defeat the affair had become a rebellion and could not be ignored.

The first response from the King's Council came on Saturday, July 13, when one Grove, a Pursuivant, arrived with a commission from the King "directed to Mr. Watson, for a reformation of divers things."[3] For this, according to the city chamberlain's accounts, Pursuivant Grove received forty shillings. The commission was presumably the Council's answer to Edmund Pynchyn's report. Robert Watson, to whom it was addressed, was a popular and influential preacher of reformed Protestant opinions. The Council was utterly mistaken in supposing that the popularity and preaching of one man could settle the situation in Norfolk, but the attempt to achieve that end by this means is wholly consistent with Somerset's policy of lenience and rational persuasion. Watson seems to have done his best. He preached to the crowd and, along with Mayor Codd and alderman Aldrich, allowed himself to be associated with Kett's administration. He recommended a clergyman, Dr. Thomas Conyers of St. Martin's at Place, who was accepted as chaplain to the Mousehold camp. But Watson was quite unable to effect any real change in the hearts of either the rebels or their opponents, and no "reformation" emerged from his activities. The rebels eventually grew tired of his efforts and imprisoned him. This mild and wholly inappropriate response from the government, besides exhibiting Somerset's enlightened treatment of the populace, shows that the Council had as yet no idea of the gravity of affairs in Norwich. And even had they seen the dangers they had no immediate alternative at this point to methods of conciliation, for by the second week in July they had already sent two armies, Russell's and Grey's, against rebellions elsewhere, and were already unable to meet Russell's demands for reinforcements.

Pursuivant Grove seems to have delivered the commission and departed. About two days later, perhaps on July 15, the city sent another messenger to the King's Council, and was duly answered by another Herald, who arrived on July 21. It was not until the city had been attacked and taken by Kett in the presence of this second Herald that the Council finally decided upon military action. Northampton's force arrived to relieve Norwich on July 31, over three weeks after Kett's army first camped outside its walls.

10. *Kett's Administration*

The period of nearly seven weeks from July 12 to August 27 during which Kett's army was camped on Mousehold Heath is divided by the successful attack made on the city on July 21. Prior to that time an uneasy truce existed whereunder rebels and citizens mixed without violence; but afterwards the city was openly hostile territory, although it still held many of Kett's friends. The period before the attack on the city is in many ways the more interesting, for it was then that Kett had the time and facilities to begin the programme of reformed administration and social order that shows, as clearly as any written manifesto, what the rebellion hoped to achieve. After the city fell Kett's time was increasingly taken up by the purely military aspects of the situation: keeping order in Norwich, attempting to spread the rebellion to nearby towns, and preparing to meet the armies that were successively sent to rescue the city he had captured.

From the first Mousehold was not only a camp but also the seat of government for Kett's new state. Here he established courts to administer justice, held council with advisers to decide on policy, issued warrants, and drew up the list of twenty-nine demands which were sent to the King. A rudimentary system of democratic representation was soon established whereby each of the thirty-three hundreds of the county of Norfolk appears to have elected two councillors or "governors." Prefixed to the list of demands is a list of the members for twenty-four of the hundreds and one member from the adjoining county of Suffolk, a total of forty-nine names. (Presumably the nine hundreds not listed were not sufficiently represented among Kett's people to elect governors.) Robert Kett placed his own name along with those of the two governors from Forehoe, bringing the total membership of this body up to fifty. The manuscript has been damaged, however, and the original list probably contained between four and eight more names than have survived. Here is the list of members, together with the hundreds they represented:

Robert Kett, Thomas Rolff, William Kett (Forehoe)
Edmond Framingham, William Tydde (North Greenhoe)
Reynold Thurston, John Wolsey (South Erpingham)
Symond English, William Pecke (East Flegg and West Flegg)

George Blomefield, William Harrison (Launditch)
Edmond Belys, Robert Sendall (Eynesford)
Thomas Prycke, Henry Hodgekins (Humbleyard)
Richard Bevis, William Doughty (North Erpingham)
Thomas Garrod, William Peter (Taverham)
Robert Manson, Robert Ede (Brothercross)
John Spregey, Eli Hill (Blofield)
John Kitball, Thomas Clerk (Walsham)
John Harper, Richard Lyon (Tunstead)
Edward Joy, Thomas Clock (Happing)
William Mow, Thomas Holling (Henstead)
John Bossell, Valentine Moore (Holt)
Robert Lerold, Richard Ward (Loddon and Clavering)
Edward Byrd, Thomas Tudenham (South Greenhoe)
Symond Newell, William Howling (Mitford)
William Heydon, Thomas Jacker (Freebridge Lynn)
Robert Cott, John Oxwick (Gallow)
William Brown, Symond Sendall (Depwade)
Richard Wright (Suffolk)[1]

This list survives on the table of demands, but there is no reason to suppose these elected governors served only to draw up that document: they almost certainly constituted a temporary "parliament" advising Kett on matters of policy.

Kett must also have had other assistants – at least a few scholars and clergymen to help with the drafting of formal papers, some of which Kett issued in Latin. One of the men whom we know served the rebels in a clerical capacity was Thomas Godsalve, son of Sir John Godsalve, Controller of the Mint. Early in the proceedings Godsalve was captured and taken to Mousehold where he was made to write out and probably aid in the composition of the documents issued by Kett and his council.

Kett also caused to be associated with him in the conduct of affairs several of the leading men of the city: in particular Mayor Codd, alderman Thomas Aldrich, and the preacher Robert Watson. These men even took precedence over the elected representatives of the hundreds, for the signatures of Codd and Aldrich appear with Kett's own at the end of the list of demands and not at the beginning with the names of the governors. One or more of their names is usually found along with Kett's on the warrants and proclamations emanating from the camp. That respected, experienced officials of city government should have been prominent members of Kett's council is at first surprising, but given that both sides genuinely wished to keep order and avoid conflict, at least for a time, this was a natural and rational state of affairs. The city gained a voice in Kett's council and was therefore able to defend its own interests without public confrontations with the camp: the appearance of cooperation would help keep in check the many in the city who sympathised with Kett and who would have been troublesome had the city tried to stand openly against the rebels. Kett gained a covering of authority for the actions of his council in so far as it included the Mayor, city aldermen, and Watson, the bearer of the King's commission to carry out reforms. His men also profited from good relations with the city, for at this time they seem to have been free to enter Norwich when they pleased and to enjoy its amenities.

From their subsequent conduct it is clear that Codd, Aldrich, and Watson had no real sympathy with the rebellion and that in subscribing to the pronouncements of Kett's council they were acting only to maintain peace and public order. They cannot have failed to see, moreover, that in so trying to keep a balance between the two sides they ran a serious risk of incurring the suspicions of both. In the event all mediation and compromise ended when Kett took the city, and on the next day, July 22, he imprisoned his three former councillors, Codd, Aldrich, and Watson, along with several other prominent citizens, and held them as hostages to ensure the good behaviour of their fellows. It is not clear how rigorous this imprisonment was, and it does not appear to have meant the end of city representation on Kett's council. A number of the citizens asked Aldrich to persuade Kett to release Codd, presumably as a sign of goodwill and to ease tensions in the city. Kett agreed, but Codd preferred not to return to Norwich, fearing that Kett's followers would become disorderly and take reprisals on the chief representative of local authority. Codd therefore stayed with Kett and may have continued as a councillor. Aldrich certainly did so, for his signature appears on the commission sent to Yarmouth from Mousehold two weeks after his imprisonment.

Thomas Aldrich evidently had more influence over Kett than any of the other city officers. He was probably the oldest among them and, having been involved in the city administration for at least fifty-two years (he was a sheriff of Norwich as early as 1497), he was easily the most experienced. He had been Mayor in 1507 and 1516, and in 1511 and 1518 he had travelled to London to represent the city council at hearings of disputes between the city and the Priory of Norwich. His residence was Mangreen Hall in Swardestone, some four miles south of Norwich, and he must therefore have been known to the Ketts and to many of their followers, for his house was only some seven miles from Wymondham. In 1549 he can hardly have been less than seventy-five years of age, and may have been more, yet he was to live another ten years after the rising. He was a very wealthy man, having been found at the assessment of 1525 to be the second richest man in Norwich.

The extent to which the delegates and other councillors participated in the formation of policy and in the administration of justice on Mousehold is uncertain. The very extent to which policies were formed and judicial procedures followed is itself a matter of doubt. There is evidence for both a high degree of order and discipline among the rebels and for a serious lack of planning and control. There is no doubt, however, that an appearance of government and regularity was carefully cultivated in imitation, as far as was possible, of the proceedings of lawfully constituted authorities. Kett's men did not rob and avenge themselves at will but obtained goods under warrant from their leaders and tried their prisoners in public. The executive officers themselves bore (forged) commissions naming them justices of the peace. Kett evidently attempted to recreate in his reformed state the essential legal, judicial, and military institutions of England. The camp also appears to have accepted without question the doctrines of the reformed Anglican Church, for they took as their chaplain Dr. Thomas Conyers, a strongly evangelical Protestant, who was to read on Mousehold twice a day services from Cranmer's new Book of Common Prayer. With these institutions necessarily went a small bureaucracy or secretariat whose task was to produce in due form the warrants and commissions and probably keep some sort of record of official acts and decisions. Accounts based on eye-witness generally emphasize the violence and disorder of the rebels, but this is inevitable since these accounts come from persons unsympathetic to the rebellion, to whom the actions of Kett's men appeared arbitrary and illegal. Kett's law was not to them law at all. The probability of some kind of regular government on Mousehold is suggested by the evidence which survives of Kett's bureaucracy and by the fact that a crowd of over ten thousand held together in one place and with one accord for over six weeks.

In order to maintain his force on Mousehold from the second week in July to the last week in August Kett must have achieved at least two feats of administration. He must first have arranged for the provisioning and adequate comforts of a very large crowd of people living on an exposed and bleak tract of land. Failure in this would inevitably have brought widespread mutiny or desertion, neither of which seems to have happened. The successful provisioning of his army, however, would not have been sufficient: these people had come, often from some distance, in order to make a protest and effect a change, and they would not be satisfied unless they could see this being done. By merely maintaining a camp on Mousehold they were achieving none of their purposes. No doubt many in Kett's army were there because conditions on the heath were better for them than conditions elsewhere: with Kett they found food, companionship, and freedom from persecution. What little we know of the composition of the army, however, indicates that most of its members were small farmers, tradesmen, or businessmen, who were losing crops and earnings, as well as endangering life and family, by joining the rebellion. Such men would not have been content to camp and feast on Mousehold in the absence of any constraining enemy force unless they could see day by day that something of their collective purpose was being effected.

The problem of satisfying the material needs of the army was at first easily solved. Kett and his lieutenants must have found accommodation in Surrey House while we know that many of the men built rough shacks from the timbers of nearby Thorpe Wood. (When the rebels moved from Mousehold on August 26 they burnt these dwellings as a sign of their intention not to return. Writing two centuries later Blomefield attributed the disappearance of Thorpe Wood to the rebels' need for building materials and fuel.[2]) Provisions were drawn from the countryside by the obvious expedient of sending out raiding parties to secure them. A degree of order and policy is indicated in the way in which this was accomplished, for Kett issued warrants to the parties concerned, punished those who exceeded the authority of the warrants or who were caught withholding goods obtained under warrant, and attempted to limit the depredations to the estates of the gentry. Here is the text of one such warrant, surprisingly issued in Latin:

> Nos Regis amici ac Delegati: pecoris et cujusvis generis commeatus conquirendi, necnon in castra Mousholdica deferendi potestatem omnibus concedimus, quocunque in loco deprehenderint, dummodo ne qua vis aut injuria honesto ac pauperi cuipiam inferatur. Cunctis ex imperio denuntiantes, prout honori ac Majestati Regiae, Reique publicae afflictae, provisum et consultum volunt, nobis Delegatis, et his quorum nomina subsequuntur dicto audientes esse.
>
> (We, the King's friends and deputies, do grant license to all men to provide and bring into the camp at Mousehold all manner of cattle and provision of vittels, in what place soever they may find the same, so that no violence or injury be done to any honest or poor man: commanding all persons, as they tender the King's honour and royal majesty, and the relief of the Commonwealth, and to those whose names ensue.)[3]

The degree of central control implied in this document is considerable. The question is how far such forms were merely a pretentious cover for robbery and terrorization. Any band of several thousand would have to do as Kett's men did in living off the surrounding countryside, and in so doing they would inevitably delegate foraging parties, attempt to ensure that all goods captured were duly surrendered to the common store, and try to avoid antagonizing sections of the populace upon whose sympathies they depended. Kett's elaborate warrants can be seen either as a rather naive attempt to cover necessary actions with a veneer of legality or as one aspect of the orderly idealism of the Norfolk rebellion.

In this way food was brought to the camp. Military supplies were also acquired, showing that although for the moment Kett had established a truce with the city he was well aware that eventual battle was inevitable. Cannon were obtained from other Norfolk towns – Sotherton mentions Lynn and Yarmouth as contributors, although it is unlikely in either case that anything was sent with official approval since both places later closed their gates against the rebels. Paston Hall, some fifteen miles north of Norwich, the original seat of the Paston family and still their property in 1549, was forced to yield more guns. Norwich itself was made to supply the powder which later helped to breach its walls.

Kett's famous court of justice held at the Oak of Reformation probably had its origins in the arrangements for receiving these provisions and supplies. To ensure fairness and general satisfaction the stores brought back to Mousehold would be delivered and distributed publicly and (it being mid summer) in the open air. The Oak of Reformation was perhaps first chosen as the central point of delivery and distribution of food, arms, and supplies. The same place would naturally be used to settle disputes regarding these goods and to hear charges against persons accused of appropriating them. A slight extension of its function makes the Oak the place in which Kett and his officers might hear complaints against their men or against prisoners brought into the camp.

Kett's court brings us to the second aspect of his administration: the public pursuit of redress of grievances. Already on the march to Mousehold several prominent local men had been taken prisoner. Others soon joined them. By continuing to accumulate prisoners from the landlords and lawyers Kett could at once begin an active implementation of reformist policies. By trying these prisoners in public Kett could demonstrate to his followers that vigorous steps were being taken to redress their grievances and bring their oppressors to account.

Sotherton gives a graphic description of judicial proceedings on Mousehold:

> and the gentlemen they took they brought to the tree of reformation to be seen of the people to demand what they would

> do with them: where some cried 'Hang him' and some 'Kill him' and some that heard no word cried even as the rest, even when themselves being demanded why they cried answered for that their fellows afore did the like, and indeed they did press their weapons to kill some of those gentlemen brought to them, which they did of such malice that one Mr. Wharton being guarded with a lane of men on both sides from the said tree into the city they pricked him with their spears and other weapons on purpose to kill him had they not had great help to withstand their malice and cruelty, and further the rest of the gentlemen imprisoned they fettered with chains and locks and appointed divers to ward them for escaping, and in the meantime with Kett's authority both constables and other officers enforced with their company to keep the gates that the citizens should not so fast range forth the city as also that no gentleman should escape.

Sotherton emphasizes the element of mob violence in the capture and trial of prisoners and although it is possible that he tells no more than the truth there is no record of serious violence against the prisoners – which indicates that the army was restrained by Kett's judicial procedures and effectively bound by his judgments.

From the nature of Kett's administration on Mousehold certain general conclusions can be drawn. That the army established courts of justice and hauled in for trial numbers of local magnates shows that much of their concern was with what they saw as the maladministration of the law in Norfolk. No doubt there were some laws they would have changed. They did not, however, challenge the general institutions of English law but tried, on the contrary, to imitate and preserve them. That the persons tried and condemned by Kett's courts were all, as far as we know, landlords or lawyers suggests that particular grievance was attached to the laws concerning real property and to the administration of justice. The fact that those condemned were sentenced to imprisonment, and not simply hanged, suggests Kett's concern to reform the law rather than to overthrow it.

The essentially local nature of the rebellion is exhibited in its concern to bring to trial the landowners and lawyers of Norfolk. The grievances of Kett's people appear not to have been strongly generalized but to have been directed against particular oppressors in particular places. Although there were no doubt many in the camp who felt that what they were doing in Norfolk should be done throughout England – as was indeed demanded in the document sent to the King – this feeling was never strong enough to generate action. The rebellion remained a Norfolk affair which succeeded in crossing only one county boundary, that of Suffolk, and even there found no lasting foothold. The body of Kett's army, and probably Kett himself, saw their immediate task as the redress of local wrongs. Nothing shows this more clearly than their initial decision to march northeastwards to Norwich instead of southwestwards to London. Even when Norwich was theirs and their numbers exceeded ten thousand they made no further move. The western rebels had begun with the intention of marching on the capital: Kett had less than half their distance to travel, could have expected an easier journey, and led a much larger force, yet so far as we know the possibility of taking the Norfolk rebellion to London was never seriously considered. The western rebellion, with its primarily religious concerns, naturally expressed itself as an attempt to influence national policy, but the Norfolk rebellion, which seems to have grown out of a host of local quarrels, was concerned with national policy only in so far as this had to be changed in order to settle the affairs of the county. The causes of the Norfolk rising lie largely in social, economic, and political conditions which pertained in most of the country, but its activities were confined to areas within about twenty miles of Norwich.

The Norfolk rising was very conservative. It aimed to preserve the institutions of the state against recent corruptions, not to overthrow or alter them in pursuit of some new ideal. We see this in Kett's concern to recreate the forms of law and in the professions of loyalty made with evident sincerity by the rebels whenever addressed by a bearer of royal authority. Most of the rebels evidently saw themselves as protectors of the law rather than as criminals. It may be wondered how a group which terrorized the local gentry and confiscated moveable property at will can be characterized as conservative. The confiscation of property, however, was necessary to the continuance of the rebels' administration: they stole in order to provision their force, and they considered their loot as nothing other than their stipend for onerously undertaking the reform of local corruptions. (They even proposed that the local gentry should be made to pay them in addition fourpence per man per day for the services rendered on Mousehold.) Nowhere is there any suggestion that Kett intended any permanent redistribution of property or any radical reform of proprietory laws. Even the fences overthrown were in theory, if not always in fact, enclosing lands to which the commons had long-established rights. Particular landowners were imprisoned by Kett for particular offences against what he understood the law to be, but no challenge to the institution of landed property or to the sixteenth-century social hierarchy emerges from Kett's rebellion.

11. *The Twenty-nine Demands*

The evidence of Kett's aims and intentions provided by his actual conduct of affairs on Mousehold is in some ways stronger than the more detailed evidence found in the twenty-nine demands sent to the King. The demands are indeed specific, and many of them extend into areas which could not be represented in Kett's limited model state on the heath, but for several reasons the demands must be regarded with some suspicion as indications of the purposes of the rebels. The document inevitably represents ideals, not all of which were practicable. It must have been drawn up by a relatively small number of the rebels and may therefore reflect at least some matters of minority interest among them while neglecting other areas of widespread concern. The list of demands, moreover, bears the signs of having been written in haste. The twenty-nine articles do not yield a coherent programme but only offer a random list of grievances ranging from such diverse particulars as fishing rights and the growth of saffron to general matters of legal and social reform. They are not, in the one surviving manuscript, presented in any special order, and their number is of no significance because some articles cover several different points while closely related issues are sometimes treated in different articles.

Here is the text, which in the manuscript follows the names of the governors and is signed beneath by Kett, Codd, and Aldrich.

> 1. We pray your grace that where it is enacted for inclosing that it be not hurtfull to such as have enclosed saffron grounds for they be greatly chargeable to them, and that from henceforth no man shall enclose any more.
> 2. We certifie your grace that whereas the lords of the manors have been charged with certain free rent, the same lords have sought means to charge the freeholders to pay the same rent, contrary to right.
> 3. We pray your grace that no lord of no manor shall common upon the commons.
> 4. We pray that priests from henceforth shall purchase no lands neither free nor bond, and the lands that they have in possession may be letten to temporal men, as they were in the first year of the reign of King Henry VII.

5. We pray that reedground and meadowground may be at such price as they were in the first year of King Henry VII.
6. We pray that all the marshes that are held of the King's majesty by free rent or of any other, may be again at the price that they were in the first year of King Henry VII.
7. We pray that all bushells within your realm be of one stice, that is to say, to be in measure viii gallons.
8. We pray that priests or vicars that be not able to preach and set forth the word of God to his parishioners may be thereby put from his benefice, and the parishioners there to chose another or else the patron or lord of the town.
9. We pray that the payments of castleward rent, and blanch farm, and office lands, which hath been accustomed to be gathered of the tenaments, whereas we suppose the lords ought to pay the same to their bailiffs for their rents gathering, and not the tenants.
10. We pray that no man under the degree of a knight or esquire keep a dove house, except it hath been of an old ancient custom.
11. We pray that all freeholders and copyholders may take the profits of all commons, and there to common, and the lords not to common nor take profits of the same.
12. We pray that no feodary within your shores shall be a counsellor to any man in his office making, whereby the King may be truly served, so that a man being of good conscience may be yearly chosen to the same office by the commons of the same shire.
13. We pray your grace to take all liberty of leet into your own hands whereby all men may quietly enjoy their commons with all profits.
14. We pray that copyhold land that is unreasonable rented may go as it did in the first year of King Henry VII and that at the death of a tenant or of a sale the same lands to be charged with an easy fine as a capon or a reasonable sum of money for a remembrance.
15. We pray that no priest [shall be a chaplain] nor no other officer to any man of honour or worship but only to be resident upon their benefices whereby their parishioners may be instructed with the laws of God.
16. We pray that all bond men may be made free for God made all free with his precious blood shedding.
17. We pray that rivers may be free and common to all men for fishing and passage.
18. We pray that no man shall be put by your escheator and feodary to find any office unless he holdeth of your grace in chief or capite above £10 a year.

19. We pray that the poor mariners and fishermen may have the whole profits of their fishings as porpoises, grampuses, whales, or any great fish so it be not prejudicial to your grace.

20. We pray that every proprietory parson or vicar having a benefice of £10 or more by year shall either by themselves or by some other person teach poor men's children of their parish the book called the catechism and the primer.

21. We pray that it be not lawful to the lords of any manor to purchase lands freely and to let them out again by copy of court roll to their great advantage and to the undoing of your poor subjects.

22. We pray that no proprietory parson or vicar in consideration of avoiding trouble and suit between them and their poor parishioners which they daily do proceed and attempt shall from henceforth take for the full contentacon of all the tenths which now they do receive but viiid. of the noble in the full discharge of all other tithes.

23. [We pray that no man] under the degree of [esquire] shall keep any conies upon any of their own freehold or copyhold unless he pale them in so that it shall not be to the commons. nuisance.

24. We pray that no person of what estate, degree, or condition he be shall from henceforth sell the awardship of any child but that the same child if he live to his full age shall be at his own chosing concerning his marriage the King's wards only except.

25. We pray that no manner of person having a manor of his own shall be no other lord's bailiff but only his own.

26. We pray that no lord, knight, nor gentleman shall have or take in farm any spiritual promotion.

27. We pray your grace to give license and authority by your gracious commission under your great seal to such commissioners as your poor commons hath chosen, or to as many of them as your majesty and your council shall appoint and think meet, for to redress and reform all such good laws, statutes, proclamations, and all other your proceedings, which hath been bidden by your Justices of your peace, Sheriffs, Escheators, and others your officers, from your poor commons, since the first year of the reign of your noble grandfather King Henry the seventh.

28. We pray that those your officers that hath offended your grace and your commons and so proved by the complaint of your poor commons do give unto these poor men so assembled ivd. every day so long as they have remained there.

29. We pray that no lord, knight, esquire, nor gentleman do graze nor feed any bullocks or sheep if he may spend forty

pounds a year by his lands but only for the provision of his house.[1]

The categories which dominate the list are partly those we would expect on the basis of the policies openly adopted by Kett on Mousehold: the laws governing property, abuses of the law by officials and landlords, and economic hardships suffered by the lower orders. There are also several other issues which, from their very nature, could not have been addressed actively by Kett's army, such as the condition of the priesthood and inflation, but most of these relate in an obvious way to the primary concern for the common man's rights to the use of land, to reasonable rents, and to equitable administration of the laws of real property.

Six articles, numbers 4, 8, 15, 20, 22, and 26, stand out as concerned with the priesthood. Two of these are really about property, aiming to prevent the clergy from enriching themselves unduly: article 4 prohibits priests from holding land, and article 22 prevents them from claiming more in tithes than they have customarily received. A secondary motive in both these articles is to keep the clergy from becoming engrossed in worldly affairs at the expense of their spiritual duties. Along with articles 8, 15, 20, and 26, they undertake a reform of the priesthood aimed to ensure that each priest is a proper man capable of his duties and not permitted to use his privileged position in order to win worldly advantage. Articles 15 and 26 object to the control of benefices by lay patrons, the gentry and aristocracy, who would appoint priests who would in fact be servants of the patron rather than of the parishes to which they were appointed. Article 8 adds that priests appointed to parishes must be competent to their task of teaching the gospel by preaching. Article 20 would ensure that those priests who have an income in excess of £10 per annum should be compelled to finance parish schools. Together this group of six articles aims to limit the material wealth of the priesthood and to enforce their performance of basic parochial duties.

These six articles pertain to the clergy but not to the church or its doctrines. There is no indication that the people of Norfolk were dissatisfied with the ecclesiastical and dogmatic reforms begun under Henry VIII and continuing under Somerset and Cranmer. On the contrary, they willingly accepted reformist Protestant preachers such as Watson and Conyers, attended services in the Norwich churches, and allowed churchmen such as Matthew Parker (a future Archbishop of Canterbury) to address them on Mousehold. The eastern rebellion, unlike that in the west, appears to have been satisfied with the government's policies on ecclesiastical and doctrinal matters. The reforms of the clergy suggested in the six articles are reasonable, and in two instances at least – the requirements that priests should preach and teach the catechism in their parishes – Kett's demands are anticipated by the injunctions issued under secretary Thomas Cromwell over ten years before.

The eastern counties were usually ahead of the government in adopting Protestant reforms. In the next century these areas were to bind together as the Eastern Association and to become strong supporters of the Puritan element in the Civil Wars. There were indeed a number of distinguished Norfolk families, such as the Jerninghams of Costessey and the Bedingfields of Oxborough, who remained Catholic and never accepted the Henrician reformation, but these were a small minority in the county. Most of the gentry and the populace were strongly Protestant in 1549.

Under Henry VIII Norfolk had produced a number of Protestant heretics but no Catholic martyrs of note. The most important was Thomas Bilney, a friend of Matthew Parker and Hugh Latimer, who was burnt in Norwich in 1531 for denying the mediation of saints. Bilney seems to have had some following in East Anglia, for Blomefield records that in 1538 "John Lambert, alias Nicholson, who was born and brought up in Norfolk, being first converted by Mr. Bilney, was burnt in Smithfield: and about the same time, Will. Layton or Leyton, a monk of Eye in Suffolk, was burnt here [Norwich], for speaking against a certain idol, which was accustomed to be carried about in processions at Eye, and for holding that the sacrament ought to be administered in both kinds."[2] A number of other cases of Norfolk Protestantism have been recorded in Henry's reign: John Church of Yarmouth denied the Catholic teaching concerning the sacraments, Thomas Baker of Sprowston refused auricular confession, and Thomas Bingy was burnt in Norwich in 1511 for denying the Pope's authority.[3] A number of these cases can be traced to the teachings of the Lollards, which may also be reflected in some of Kett's demands – such as that priests should be preachers and that clerical property should be curtailed.

Kett's men were content with the Henrician reformation and with the doctrinal and liturgical reforms currently proceeding under Archbishop Cranmer. The new book of Common Prayer, use of which became mandatory on June 9, 1549, was regularly used in Conyers' services in Mousehold. Had the eastern rising been seriously concerned to combat Protestant innovations it would hardly have failed to turn to Princess Mary, heir presumptive to the throne and an avowed Catholic, who was at that time residing in the former Howard mansion at Kenninghall only eleven miles from Wymondham. The rebels totally ignored Mary, just as in their demands they ignored doctrinal issues, because they were largely satisfied with the pace and direction of current religious reforms.

By far the largest group of articles, at least seventeen out of the twenty-nine, are concerned with land – with common rights to land and water, with rents and land prices, and with the laws governing landed property and tenancy. Only one article, the first, mentions enclosures, and does so, moreover, in a strange way, saying first that enclosures made for the better cultivation of saffron should not be disallowed and adding, almost as an afterthought, that no further enclosures should be permitted. The growth of saffron was an important local industry necessary to the manufacture of worstead, which explains Kett's willingness to let stand the fences round the saffron fields. But it is still surprising that the rebellion, which began as a riot against enclosures, should begin its list of demands by asking the government not to implement the anti-enclosure proclamations in certain cases, and should then make no further references to enclosures in the remaining articles.

Article 1 is the only one which mentions enclosures as such, but a number of the other articles deal with activities closely related to enclosure, such as the pasturing of large herds on common land (articles 29, 3, and 11), the conversion of freehold land to copyhold (article 21), and forcing a poor farmer into expensive legal battles in order to gain control of his land (article 18). With enclosure in the strict sense of the erection of fences around common land Kett's demands have little to do, but enclosure in this narrow sense was only one aspect of the changing economic situation. The term enclosure is usually used more widely and covers a multitude of sins all tending to increase the landholdings of the gentry at the expense of the poor farmer. A considerable number of the articles are concerned with enclosure in this larger sense.

The landlords did not have to build fences and cut off traditional rights of access in order to effect their ends. They could, quite legally, assert their own rights to use the common lands. Because their herds would be much larger than those of their poorer neighbours the result would be much the same as if they had appropriated the fields to their own exclusive uses. Article 3 aims to exclude the lord of the manor from the common lands, article 11 asserts the exclusive common rights of freeholders and copyholders, and article 29 forbids anyone whose lands are worth more than £40 per annum from keeping flocks or herds larger than were needed for the consumption of his own household. The last of these articles is most far-reaching: in effect it places an upper limit on the size of sheep and cattle farms. This article alone "would have clipped the wings of rural capitalism."[4]

The lord of the manor could use other means to aggrandize his holdings. He could, for instance, buy up freehold land whenever possible and in subsequently letting it convert it to copyhold. He was able to do this by virtue of his feudal position as lord and through his control of the manorial courts and of the court rolls wherein copyhold was often recorded. In this way, in due time, large blocks of copyhold land could be created and at this point, again through the manorial courts if necessary, the lord could bring pressure to bear upon the copyholders to extort their consent to enclosure. Kett's demands include a prohibition on the conversion of freehold land to copyhold (article 21) and a request for the abolition of courts leet (article 13).

The law could be used in various ways to drive even the small freeholder off his property. Two officers with exceptional legal powers in matters of real property were the escheator and the feodary. The escheator was the county officer responsible for lands forfeit in any way to the Crown, and the feodary was another such officer, a representative of the Court of Wards, responsible for lands held from the Crown by knight service. Either of these officers could make legal demands of any landowner, fulfilment of which might well prove beyond the means of many. Article 18 demands immunity from these requirements for all whose lands are worth less than £10 per annum.

Another way in which the lords appear to have been taking advantage of their tenants was by forcing them to bear taxes and expenses which should have been met by the lords themselves. Articles 2 and 9 protest against such practices. Article 14 makes a general complaint against rising rents, which reminds us that all the economic clauses of the document must be read in the light of the severe inflation of the period. Besides the three articles just mentioned pertaining to rents and tenants' dues, two more, articles 5 and 6, object directly to the high prices of land. Other articles, such as 4 and 12, are indirectly concerned with the land market. The amassing of lands by the church had been a grievance for many centuries, apparently answered by the dissolution of the monasteries. Ten years after the dissolution, however, it was clear that one generally beneficient landlord had been replaced by a class of generally selfish new-made gentry, and that nothing had been done to make land more available to the small farmer. Article 4 aims to keep priests from bidding for what little free land there was, and article 12 is presumably intended to prevent the feodary from abusing his position as agent for Crown lands in the county.

This takes care of a large group of articles concerned with the ownership, use, and purchase of land, the largest group of articles in the document and evidently the primary concern of its authors. Three more should probably be considered in relation to these: article 25, which asks that no lord of a manor should act as bailiff to another landlord, and articles 17 and 19, both concerned with the rights of fishermen. Article 17 is directed against what amounts to enclosure of the waterways. Article 19 asks the crown to relinquish its rights over "fishes royal" such as porpoises, grampuses, and whales.

Of the remaining articles two more, 10 and 23, are designed to safeguard the property of the small farmer. The keeping of dovecotes and rabbit warrens was a luxury which the wealthy could afford but which was much resented by their poorer neighbours whose crops were frequently despoiled by the doves and rabbits. The rebels' dislike of dovecotes had already been expressed when they destroyed that recently established by John Corbet of Sprowston. Both these articles are moderate in tone, the one prohibiting the building of new dovecotes but not challenging the old ones, and the other leaving open the right to keep rabbits provided they are fenced in.

Two isolated articles, unrelated to the others or to one another, are 7, which requests the enforcement of a national standard of measure, and 24, which aims to limit the powers of guardians to arrange marriages for their wards – a power frequently exercised to the guardian's own financial advantage. The King, who profited most from wardship as the guardian of all children of deceased noblemen, is interestingly excepted from article 24.

Three significant articles are still outstanding. One of these, article 27, makes a general plea for a commission to enforce laws made since the accession of Henry VII. The demand is not for law reform but for the enforcement of existing laws, which suggests that in general Kett's men approved of Tudor legislation. The document does contain requests for some changes of law on particular matters, but it is much more strongly concerned to secure the equitable administration of the law as it stood. Several articles, including this one, imply various malpractices on the part of legal officers such as sheriffs, justices, feodaries, and escheators. (It can hardly be coincidence that the escheator for Norfolk in 1548 was John Flowerdew.) Because their programme coincided largely with the policies actually pursued by Somerset the rebels saw themselves not as agitators hostile to the government but as agents carrying out the government's intentions in the face of a conspiracy of local landlords. Hence the claim in article 28 that those giving their time to the business transacted on Mousehold should be paid for their services. This explains why the rebellion was a local one and never took the form of a march on the capital: the rebels' quarrel was not with Somerset or the King but with local lawyers and gentry who withheld and perverted the King's justice.

The most striking article is 16, which appears to assert social egalitarianism on a basis of Christian idealism. The freedom claimed for all men, however, does not imply social equality, for all Englishmen were already free except only those who were still in the state of villeinage – those who were bound to give their labour at certain times each year to their lords. At one time, in the years immediately after the Norman Conquest, the greater part of the native (non-Norman) population were in this state, but over the centuries since then most men had won or purchased freedom, until by the mid sixteenth century those whom the law would still call villeins were a very small minority. There could have been only a few hundred such in the whole of Norfolk,[5] and even these were not seriously burdened by their status since the courts by this date were not enforcing the lords' claims on the services of villeins. In a case of 1552 from Gimingham in Norfolk it was ruled that the tenants should be permitted to compound for the services due.[6] It would be a mistake to see article 16 as the main demand to which the others are subservient appendages: the freedom claimed was a technical legal status of which all but a very few were already possessed. Article 16 is not a radical assertion of human dignity but an objection to an archaic survival from feudal law which had long since fallen into virtual disuse.

The list of demands exhibits the same qualities of conservatism and localization that we observed in Kett's active policies on Mousehold. Although the main problems addressed by the list were to be found almost throughout England quite a number of the articles have a distinctly local flavour expressed in references to the growing of saffron, to reedbeds and marshes, and to fishing rights. Several articles, in the light of what is known, derive from local events and personalities: the escheator, who is mentioned twice, is surely Sergeant Flowerdew, and the dovecote may well be that destroyed in Sprowston. The conservatism of the document is evident in several ways, especially in the desire expressed in four articles to return to the way things were under Henry VII. The list of demands is not a radical document: its general tenor is that existing laws should be enforced and current policies pursued. This same conservatism ensured that Kett's rebellion would remain a local phenomenon. Agreeing as it did with the King's government Kett's rising could not seek a national revolution: of necessity, therefore, it vented its anger against subordinate officers and magnates who, it was claimed, were interfering in particular places with the implementation of the government's policies.

The most striking general conclusion to be drawn from the twenty-nine articles is that their primary concerns are those of men of moderate but sufficient means – concerns for the price of land, for the right to graze herds and flocks on the common land, for the right to farm one's land without fear of eviction or unreasonable fees and rents. Very few of the articles are directly relevant to the lot of the destitute pauper, of whose kind it has been suggested that Kett's band was largely composed. It is true that the number of beggars had increased dramatically as a result of rising rents and enclosures in the decades before the rebellion, and it may be that many such persons joined Kett's company; but the list of demands has little bearing on their plight. The articles represent the interests of men who already have a place in society and who would like a somewhat larger one, not of the outcast and persecuted poor who had no place and no property.

The composition of Kett's army will be forever mysterious because, for obvious reasons, no lists were kept at the time of its existence and thereafter no-one would willingly place on record the fact of his participation. In a few cases, however, the names and occupations of individual members of the camp have come down to us, and a risky generalization on the basis of this small sample suggests that the army consisted largely of small independent farmers, self-employed craftsmen, and tradesmen. Such evidence, reinforced by the nature of the demands, indicates that the rebellion was not a rising of oppressed peasants against the gentry and aristocracy but one of small farmers and businessmen against the large farmers, their lawyers, and their control of the courts and markets.

12. *Matthew Parker*

At some time during the first week of their occupation of the heath Kett's men were visited by Matthew Parker. A little over ten years later Parker became Archbishop of Canterbury and subsequently prompted one of his junior secretaries, Alexander Neville, to write an account of the Norfolk rising, presumably supplying Neville with much of the necessary information. Neville's *De furoribus Norfolciensium Ketto duce*, published in 1575 (the year of Parker's death), is the most important source for the events of the rebellion after the eyewitness account of Nicholas Sotherton.

Parker's grandfather, Nicholas Parker, had been registrar to Archbishop Bourchier of Canterbury. His father, William Parker, had settled in Norwich as a worstead weaver sometime before Matthew's birth there in 1504. Throughout his life Matthew maintained close connections with Norfolk and with Norwich. His father died in 1516, but his younger brother Thomas still lived in the city, apparently prospering, becoming Sheriff of Norwich in 1558 and Mayor ten years later. Visiting his brother Thomas in 1549 Parker bravely took the opportunity to go to Kett's camp and preach to the rebel army.

Matthew Parker, at this time aged forty-four, was already a distinguished man with an impressive record of academic honours and ecclesiastical preferments.[1] He had entered Corpus Christi College, Cambridge, in about 1521 and was later admitted to Holy Orders. At Cambridge he was friendly with the reforming group which included Hugh Latimer and Thomas Bilney. The gentle and ascetic Bilney seems to have attracted him, for he journeyed to Norwich in 1531 to be present at the burning of the Norfolk martyr. Parker himself escaped persecution and rode on a wave of increasing good fortune when Henry VIII decided on a breach with Rome in order to secure his marriage with Anne Boleyn. Queen Anne was strongly Protestant and Parker was appointed her chaplain in 1535. He apparently pleased the King, for in spite of Anne's execution Parker retained the Deanery of the college of Stoke-by-Clare which he had been granted, and was appointed chaplain to Henry himself in 1538. In 1544 he was, by the King's command, made master of his college, Corpus Christi, of which he had been a fellow since 1527. He was elected Vice Chancellor of Cambridge in 1545 and again in 1548. He also held the livings of Burlingham in Norfolk and Landbeach in Cambridgeshire.

Such was the man who, probably on the morning of July 13, 1549, tried in a sermon to persuade Kett's army to disperse. Parker continued to rise under Edward VI, becoming Dean of Lincoln in 1552, probably after refusing a bishopric. But with the accession of the Catholic Queen Mary in 1553 he was deprived of all his offices and benefices and forced to live out the reign in retirement. Queen Elizabeth, reversing her sister's religious policies, called Parker out of seclusion on her succession, despite his own sincere disinclination, to succeed the late Cardinal Pole as Archbishop of Canterbury. He was consecrated in December, 1559, and held that difficult post until his death sixteen years later.

Parker's visit to Norwich at the time of Kett's assembly on Mousehold may have been a coincidence, but it is more likely that word had reached him in Cambridge of the disturbances in the Norwich area as a result of which he had decided to see for himself what was happening. His curiosity, if such it was, would not have been idle: not only did he have family and friends in the city but also his rectory of Burlingham was less than ten miles away. Parker was, moreover, an eager and effective preacher. There is evidence that he always felt his first duty was to preach to the common people, and it may be that he had come to Norwich on this occasion with that intention.

Parker first visited the heath, accompanied by his brother, in the evening (probably the evening of July 12). His intention was to address the people there and then, but what he found when he arrived caused him to delay the sermon until the following morning. He found Kett and his people engaged in a heated debate over the unfortunate person of Mayor Codd, whom many there felt should resign but who was steadfastly refusing to do so. (The story is puzzling because it is not clear what Kett could hope to gain by Codd's resignation – unless perhaps the surrender of the city. But if the resistance of the city really depended upon Codd alone then that officer possessed far greater strength of character than he has been given credit for.) At the same time, according to Neville, the majority of the people were overcome with a surfeit of eating and drinking, so that those who were not occupied with the Mayor were in no condition to hear a sermon. Under these circumstances Parker wisely decided to save his address for the cold sobriety of morning and returned to the city, no doubt to spend a comfortable night in his brother's house.

Parker's account (through Neville) of the army's high living is seriously to their discredit, for it is hardly consistent with the picture Kett's men presented of themselves as the King's agents for the restoration of law and social order. For all his integrity, however, Parker is a hostile witness: he came to Mousehold to persuade the army to disperse and, as we shall see, was not well treated for his trouble. He could hardly be expected to describe the rebels sympathetically, especially fifteen or so years later when, as Archbishop, he retold the story for Neville's publication. Moreover, if his first visit to the heath was indeed on the evening of July 12 the rebels themselves had only just arrived there and what Parker saw as the effects of debauchery could well have been relaxation and exhaustion after several days of unsettled marching and camping.

The scene was much more promising when Parker returned next morning. As he arrived Conyers was leading the people in prayer, and a mood appropriate to the sermon Parker had in mind was already created. He therefore addressed the crowd, taking his stand on the platform built in or around the Oak of Reformation, which served both as judicial bench and pulpit. His sermon, for which our source is his own recollection imparted to Neville many years later, made three points in particular: first it blamed the people for their intemperance, which Parker believed he had witnessed the evening before; secondly it warned them not to shed blood or indulge in private feuds; and thirdly it advised them strongly to abandon their enterprise and to trust the King's messengers. (The messengers referred to might have been Watson or sheriff Wyndham, or Parker might have been looking forward to the further emissaries who would inevitably be sent from London in the near future.) The sermon concluded with praise for the King and a plea that questions of reform be left in abeyance until Edward's majority. Parker's address thus appears to have been a reasonably diplomatic plea for moderation and patience rather than an outright condemnation of the rebels' activities. It was nonetheless brave, perhaps even rash, of him to have delivered it.

His cloth afforded him some protection. Kett's men, as we have seen, had no quarrel with the new Protestant faith to which Parker subscribed. They were in the course of devotions when he arrived and they seem to have heard him willingly. Towards the end, however, as he was advising them to disperse, to trust the King's agents, and to postpone their demands, there was increasing unrest in his audience. Finally the crowd took up the notion that Parker had been paid or prompted by the landlords to persuade them to disperse, and their behaviour thereupon became distinctly menacing. Parker was apparently poked and prodded with sticks and spears as he stood somewhat above the people on the platform. An ugly situation was resolved by the presence of mind of Conyers who, having three or four choristers with him, ıp the *Te Deum*. The crowd was diverted by the music and ook the opportunity to make a discrete withdrawal.

: was heading for the Pockthorpe Gate Parker was n by several of Kett's men who, presumably angered by ᵖposition that he might be an agent of the landlords, demanded to see his license to preach. Parker had been licensed to preach in 1533 by Archbishop Cranmer, but it is doubtful whether there on Mousehold he could have produced evidence to satisfy his accusers. Fortunately his brother Thomas was with him and managed somehow to engage the rebels in argument while Parker completed his escape into the city.

The story of Parker's intervention in the Norfolk rising does not end there but has an amusing sequel. On the next day Parker preached in the church of St. Clement in Norwich. This was therefore probably a Sunday, in which case it would have been either July 14 or July 21. But it is unlikely to have been July 21 because we know that on that day the whole situation in Norwich was altered by the arrival of a herald from the King, whereas everything in Parker's story suggests that nothing had been heard from London since Watson received his commission from Pursuivant Grove. Assuming that Parker preached in St. Clement's on July 14 we can date his sermon on Mousehold as of July 13, and his first visit to the camp must then have been on the evening of July 12, the day on which the rebels themselves arrived there. Parker's attempt to disperse the rebels therefore seems to have been made early in the rebellion, only four or five days after the similar attempts of Wyndham and Wodehouse.

St. Clement's stands at the junction of Magdalen Street and Colegate just over the Fye Bridge in the northern sector of Norwich which is divided from the rest of the city by a curve in the river Wensum. The church is small and appears mostly perpendicular. Although Parker was born in the nearby parish of St. Saviour's, he was first educated by the rector of St. Clement's and probably attended St. Clement's parish school. His parents are buried there in a grave on the south side of the church now marked by a nineteenth-century reconstruction of the original memorial. When Parker faced his audience there on that Sunday morning he found among them a number of the rebels, probably still suspicious of his motives. Even so he did not refrain from preaching against the rebellion. After the service he was stopped by the rebels who demanded that the three or four horses he had with him be delivered for the King's service on Mousehold. Craftily Parker managed to gain time, agreeing to present the horses for inspection later in the day. Meanwhile he sent his servant to remove some of the horses' shoes, to pare their feet to the quick, and to paint them with nerve tonic as though they had been sick. When the horses were exhibited to the rebels they appeared lame and unhealthy and Parker was allowed to keep them.

Parker evidently felt himself still under suspicion and perhaps even surveillance. The next day, probably Monday, July 15, he went out on what was meant to seem an innocent stroll, leaving the city in the direction of Cringleford village. At Cringleford, where the road to Wymondham, Thetford, and Cambridge crosses the Yare, his servant and horses were waiting and Parker set off at once for the haven of Corpus Christi.

Parker's return to Cambridge was not necessarily a retreat. There was, in any event, nothing more he could do in Norwich, and to have stayed would possibly have endangered his own freedom and that of his family. Besides, serious riots against enclosures had occurred in the villages around Cambridge on July 10 and had been dispersed with difficulty by the Mayor and Vice Chancellor. Parker must have left Cambridge for Norwich before the riots began and he would not have heard of them until his efforts to disperse the Norfolk rebels were under way. Once it was apparent that he could do nothing useful in Norwich, however, Parker would naturally have wanted to return to Cambridge in view of the situation there. He might well have received messages from Cambridge asking him to return, for as a past Vice Chancellor and present head of a college he was an important figure in the university, which was involved in the troubles because the colleges were among the major local landlords. Parker's college, Corpus Christi, owned property in Landbeach near Cambridge, of which parish Parker had been rector since 1545. For some time past there had been contentions in Landbeach between the villagers and another landowner Richard Kirby. The matter had been taken to law but no satisfactory settlement had been reached. Through the spring and summer of 1549 there was increasing tension in the village and occasional acts of violence. As Master of the college and rector of the parish Parker had heavy responsibilities in Landbeach and it is probable that he returned to Cambridge when he did because, hearing of the riots there, he was anxious to supervise the interests of his college and his parishioners. At any rate he was actively involved in the settlement of affairs in Landbeach in the following months, so much so that it has been suggested that had he not intervened the Landbeach troubles might have spread and caused a major rising around Cambridge rather as the Wymondham riots had spread and engulfed Norwich.[2]

13. *The King's Messenger*

For some ten days after the insurgents' arrival on Mousehold an uneasy truce was observed between camp and city. The city had not the wherewithal to defy Kett and was distracted by a multitude of rebel supporters within its walls. The city policy was therefore to wait, avoiding conflict, until word should come from London. Kett appears to have observed the truce because he did not wish for the bloodshed and bitterness of a local civil war and because he hoped that the city would continue to accede to his demands: Norwich was already granting funds and supplies to the army on Mousehold and in time its weakness and internal dissensions might force it to capitulate altogether. The truce was ended by the messenger from the King's Council who arrived on Sunday, July 21. His coming committed the government to the defence of the city and in effect required a stand against the rebels to be taken. At the same time it showed Kett that the government would not support him or admit the justice of his cause, and so forced him either to fight as a declared rebel or to disband with nothing accomplished.

The city's first request for help had been answered on July 13 by Pursuivant Grove with a commission to Mr. Watson, but even before Grove arrived it was clear that stronger measures would be necessary. Shortly afterwards, probably on Monday, July 15, another messenger left for London, this time a prominent citizen, Leonard Sotherton. Leonard Sotherton was brother to Nicholas whose manuscript "The Commoyson in Norfolk 1549" is the only direct eyewitness account of Kett's rebellion. The Sothertons were a prominent Norwich family: the father of Leonard and Nicholas, Nicholas Sotherton senior, had been Mayor of the city in 1539; Leonard was Sheriff of Norwich in 1556; and the younger Nicholas was sheriff in 1572 and alderman from 1576 to his death eleven years later. In the assessment of 1576 the younger Nicholas was found to be one of the richest men in his parish. Another brother, Thomas Sotherton, was Sheriff with Leonard in 1556, was Member of Parliament for Norwich in the last year of Mary's reign, and was Mayor in 1565. The impressive tombs of the Sothertons can still be seen in the church of St. John Maddermarket.

Leonard Sotherton rode to London because the rebels had threatened him and in order to get help for the city. He reported to the King's Council and suggested that an offer of pardon might still persuade the rebels to disperse. The Council, their hands already full with rebellions in the west and the midlands, hopefully accepted Sotherton's view and sent him back in company with the York Herald bearing an official offer of pardon to Kett's men on condition of dispersal. Sotherton, who had apparently undertaken the journey to London at his own expense, had been robbed on the way there and subsequently received £2.16.8 in compensation from the city. The Herald who returned with him received eight gold sovereigns (£4).

The Herald was greeted by the city officers and given refreshments in the Council chamber. Then, preceded by John Petibone, the city swordbearer, and accompanied by other officials, the Herald set off for Mousehold. He was received with cheers and heard willingly by Kett's men as he proclaimed them rebels but offered pardon to all who would submit. Many of the crowd were moved by this, falling to their knees, crying "God save the King!" and giving thanks for royal mercy. Kett, however, felt that the Herald's message was an inappropriate response to his demands: he did not consider himself a rebel, he was sure that justice and (to a large extent at least) law were on his side, and would not accept pardon because he had committed no treason. He probably spoke to the army to this effect after the Herald had finished, and the outcome was that the great majority of his men rejected the pardon and refused to submit. It would be interesting to know what instructions if any the York Herald had been given to cover this contingency. In the event, when he was told that the army would not surrender, he turned to swordbearer Petibone and ordered the arrest of the rebels. Kett's force at this time probably numbered considerably more than ten thousand. Whether or not Petibone made any attempt to carry out the Herald's instructions the army remained intact on Mousehold and the Herald's party returned to the city accompanied by only a small number of rebels who wished to claim the offered pardon.

The party re-entered the city by the Bishopsgate bridge. At once the Mayor ordered the city gates closed and a watch kept around the walls. The Herald's coming was decisive, for his message officially declared those who remained on Mousehold to be rebels and made it the duty of every loyal subject to resist them. Codd had no real choice: once the Herald's declaration had been made the city had to dissociate itself completely from Kett's force, even although this would probably mean battle, defeat, and serious loss of life and property. The Herald had brought no force to back his threats, which made it inevitable that when the city osed its gates Kett would break them open again. Kett had no ore choice than Codd: he could not permit his army's main source of supply to defy him without a fight, especially because it must have been obvious to the rebels that Norwich could not hold out against their attack. Kett had brought his army to Norwich and now that the city had closed its gates he could not do anything but lead an assault. The Herald's proclamation precipitated a situation in which neither the city fathers nor the camp leaders had any real freedom of action. For what followed the responsibility rests largely with Somerset and the King's Council who made it impossible for the local authorities in Norwich to continue any degree of cooperation with Kett but gave them no means to resist him.

In the city Codd took what measures he could. The prisoners kept by Kett's orders in the Castle and the Guildhall jails were released, but because so many of Kett's men and their supporters were still at large in the city some prisoners decided it was safer for them to remain voluntarily in confinement. Other prisoners, however, appear to have gained their freedom and aided the city's defences: the help of Thomas Godsalve and the two Appleyard brothers, all formerly captured by Kett, is recorded in the city Chamberlain's accounts for July 21. The city cannon were placed on the Castle ditches (i.e. on the top of the high banks which formed the outer defences of the keep) on the east side facing Mousehold. Kett placed his guns on the high grounds of the heath about a mile away across the Wensum. Firing commenced in the evening and continued through the night, doing little damage on either side because the distance between them was too great.

Some particulars of the city's preparations for defence survive in the Chamberlain's accounts. Lead for shot and paper for matches were purchased, and two men employed to make the shot, which was then distributed to the gunners. A gun was brought to the common staithe yard and put in the charge of the Appleyard brothers. The two larger guns sent by Sir William Paston from Caister Castle were taken from the staithe to the high ground of the Castle ditches and there supervised by Thomas Godsalve and others. The Bishop's Gates, the most exposed point on the side of the city facing Kett, was "rampired with erth that nyght." The city's strategy was inevitably defensive. Its hope lay in holding off the rebels for several days so as to weaken Kett's army for want of supplies and to give the government time to send reinforcements.

The next day, Monday, July 22, the fighting began in earnest. Each side began by moving up its guns: the city brought its heavy guns from the Castle to the meadows beside the river and Kett brought his down from the heath. Only the river and a little open land on either side of it now lay between the two forces. Kett sent two envoys, Isaac Williams, a tailor, and Ralph Sutton, a hatter, to demand of the Mayor a right of way for Kett's men through the city whereby provisions might be brought to the camp. This may have been a sincere effort to avoid bloodshed at the last minute, but Kett must have known that the city could not back down. Codd could do nothing but send a refusal. Kett opened fire and the city guns replied.

Neither side had skilled gunners and both were short of powder: consequently the artillery achieved nothing decisive. The rebels then assaulted the gates, which were defended from within and from the walls by archers. Arrows proved ineffective against the force of the attack. Sotherton gives a vivid picture of the reckless bravery of the assault: "So impudent were they and so desperate, that their vagabond boys, naked and unarmed, came among the thickest of the arrows and gathered them up, when some of the said arrows stuck fast in their legs and other parts." The boys "plucked out the very arrows that were sticking in their bodies, and gave them, all dripping with blood, to the rebels who were standing round, to fire again at the city."

The weakest point in the defences was Bishopsgate. The bridge had a fortified gateway and earthen ramparts (hastily built up the night before), but on either side it was defended by nothing but the river. By the simple expedient of swimming across the river in considerable numbers the rebels outflanked the gate and drove off its defenders. The bridge was then open and the defences breached. The city was quickly taken.

Kett at once commandeered the city's guns and powder. One John Fishman informed him of the stores of powder and shot kept by the city chamberlain, and Kett sent a force of some eighty men to the Chamberlain's house. According to the Chamberlain's own story, set down in the accounts, this force, led by Robert Ysod, tanner, John Baker, butcher, and one Echard, a miller from Heyham (Heigham?), carried that unfortunate official from his house to the Guildhall where the stores were kept. From there they took two barrels of powder, one full and one part full, iron and lead pellets, and some pikes, and made the Chamberlain supply them with rope and baskets to carry off the booty. Later they came again to his house and took 120 bullets made the night before, along with some six pounds worth of the Chamberlain's own corn, powder, and paper. Again he was compelled to supply baskets and string to help the rebels remove the goods.

The York Herald was still in the city and his commission was still valid. When the fighting had died down he re-read his message in the market place, which was now filled with Kett's men. They, elated by their easy victory, heard him with derision, and the Herald, in some fear for his safety, desired alderman Augustine Steward to escort him from the city. Followed by a jeering crowd he left through St. Stephen's Gate and took the road for London, having unwittingly caused the capture of the city.

Having taken the city's weapons and occupied its strategic places with his own people Kett returned to Mousehold. Although they were now masters of Norwich most of the rebels continued to live on the heath. Some, no doubt, quartered themselves upon the citizens or occupied the city churches and public buildings, but the city could by no means accommodate them all. Kett must thereafter have spent most of his time in Norwich, but his headquarters remained the Oak on the heath and his residence was still Surrey House. There was, moreover, a sound strategic reason for maintaining the camp outside the city. Norwich had just proved itself vulnerable and virtually indefensible against a large scale attack. That it would be attacked again if Kett occupied it was certain, for troops would be sent as soon as the Herald delivered his report to the Council. If Kett moved into Norwich he would be as exposed to the government forces as the citizens had been to him, whereas by remaining on Mousehold he could dominate the city and retake it whenever it closed its gates.

To ensure peace until the government initiated the next stage of the struggle Kett took with him as captives most of the city's leaders, including Mayor Codd, the preacher Robert Watson, aldermen Thomas Aldrich, and William Rogers, John Humberston, William Brampton, and others. Humberston had been Sheriff of Norwich in 1538 and Rogers Sheriff in 1531, Member of Parliament in 1542, and Mayor in 1542 and 1548. These men were held prisoner in Surrey House where, according to Sotherton, they were kept in chains and where some of them died. Aldrich, one of the oldest and wealthiest of the citizens, was elected by the others to ask Kett to release the Mayor. Kett did so, presumably as a gesture of goodwill in hopes of keeping order in the city, but Codd had no wish to return to his office while the city was in the hands of the rebels. He preferred to remain in the comparative security of Surrey House, effectually under Kett's protection, and he appointed deputies to act for him in the city.

Two city officers, the Sheriffs Henry Bacon and John Atkins, appear to have retained their freedom and authority. Bacon was a wealthy merchant whose fine house still stands in Colegate not far from what remains of the house of Thomas Aldrich. He was later to be Mayor of Norwich in 1557 and 1566. The deputy Mayor, however, who in the absence of Codd, Aldrich, and Watson, seems to have led the citizens until the end of the rebellion was Augustine Steward. Steward, who had already taken up his mayoral duties in escorting the Herald from the city, was a wealthy man, by trade a mercer, whose impressive house stands in Tombland opposite the Erpingham Gate into the Cathedral Close. He had been Mayor in 1534, when he had instituted the building of the Guildhall, again in 1546, and Member of Parliament for Norwich in 1541. He was to be Mayor for the third and last time in 1556.

Steward's task was a difficult one. How the rebels and citizens conducted themselves in the wake of the battle is hard to determine. That the records are silent suggests that there was no serious damage done and no capital reprisals taken against the defenders. Some churches were desecrated – St. Bartholomew's in Ber Street, for instance, of which only the ruined tower now stands – and some of those active in the defence of the city were given many anxious moments. The city Chamberlain recorded that on July 23, the day after the battle, a hundred or more rebels came again to his house, took more arms and goods, and began taking away the Chamberlain himself in order, they said, to try him at the Oak for having organized the manufacture of shot used against them in the battle. He so pleaded with them, however, that they accepted three shillings and fourpence "for remission from going to the tree" and let him go. The case may not be typical but it shows what we would expect: the rebels were not so disciplined as to be above petty theft and the acceptance of bribes, but they were not so abandoned as to hang their opponents out of hand. The terrified Chamberlain was being taken for trial, not execution, and his sentence would have been imprisonment, almost certainly, and not death.

14. *Northampton's Army*

The York Herald must have made his report to the Council on or about July 24. Somerset acted promptly and within a week government forces were in sight of Norwich. The rejection of the offer of pardon left no alternative to suppression of the rising by force of arms, but with rebels still very much at large in the midlands and the southwest the government had few forces to dispose of at such short notice. Nonetheless Sir William Parr, Marquess of Northampton and brother to the dowager Queen Catherine, was dispatched in command of a force which numbered perhaps fifteen hundred men, including a body of Italian mercenaries. It is customary to blame the disaster which ensued upon Northampton's incompetence. He was indeed foolish in his conduct of the campaign, but it can hardly be maintained that any commander with the same small resources, outnumbered by almost ten to one, could have stood against Kett at this moment.

Parr was chosen for the task because he had the rank and because, as Lord Lieutenant of the five eastern counties, an office to which he had only just been appointed, it was properly his duty to restore order in Norfolk. He was, however, primarily a courtier and had only little military experience. As Sir William Parr he had served against the northern rebels in 1537 in the aftermath of the Pilgrimage of Grace. He was a man of good education and of some property, being the heir of his father, Sir Thomas Parr of Kendal, who had died in 1518. For his services and qualifications he was created Baron Parr of Kendal in 1539. Like Somerset, therefore, Parr began his career by winning the attention and favour of the King, but again like Somerset, he owed his sudden rise to higher rank to a sister's marriage with the King. Henry married Catherine Parr in July, 1543, and in the same year her brother was made a Privy Councillor, a member of the council of the north, a Knight of the Garter, and Earl of Essex. In the next year he served as chief captain of the men at arms on the expedition to Boulogne, his only experience of military command. Henry's will named him one of the twelve advisors to the Council of executors. He was not appointed an executor but, perhaps in compensation, was created Marquess of Northampton, a title which made him the fourth nobleman of the kingdom (after the Dukes of Suffolk and

Somerset and the Marquess of Dorset).

Up to this time Northampton had been friendly to Somerset, but was soon to be alienated from the Protector over the question of his divorce. Northampton was separated from his first wife Anne, Lady Bourchier, and having fallen in love with Elizabeth, daughter of Lord Cobham, he petitioned in 1547 that an ecclesiastical commission should determine whether or not he might divorce Anne to marry Elizabeth. In May a committee, led by Cranmer, Ridley, and Holbeach, met to debate the question, but instead of reaching a decision they felt that principles were at stake and that prolonged deliberation would be needed. Northampton grew impatient and secretly married his lady. When this was discovered he was called before the Council for contempt and ordered to separate from Elizabeth until the committee reached its decision. His divorce was eventually allowed, but not before he had been alienated from Somerset by the humiliation and inconvenience of the Council's order, for which he held the Protector responsible.

Somerset and Northampton had run similar courses under Henry. Both were sons of country gentlemen, both gained a footing at court on their own merits, and both were elevated as they became successively brothers-in-law to the King. But whereas Somerset had proved himself a soldier and a politician Northampton remained a courtier of no strong talents, and Somerset had the additional advantage of being uncle to the King's heir whereas Northampton was only the brother to his widow. Consequently Somerset wielded substantial powers in the new reign while Northampton had only rank and prestige. The situation appears not to have troubled Parr, who supported Somerset's Protectorate and gladly took a subordinate place in the enlarged Privy Council. He was probably content to let others govern so long as he himself received due respect and the privileges of his rank. The difficulty over his divorce irked him not only because he felt that the rules could easily have been waived by his colleagues on the Council but also because, by a strange coincidence, Somerset himself had committed a similar bigamy some years before. The future Protector had married Catherine Fillol whom, around 1531, he found it necessary to repudiate for infidelity. She died in 1535, but while she still lived Seymour contracted a second marriage with Anne Stanhope. Northampton no doubt felt that his own case was in essentials the same as Somerset's and resented the Protector's failure to save him from the humiliation and delay imposed by the Council and the bishops.

Perhaps for these personal reasons Northampton was ready to join Warwick against Somerset when the circumstances of the Norfolk rebellion threw the two commanders together. Parr was not a political figure of the first rank, but he was a courtier of considerable prestige. Warwick went out of his way to keep the Marquess's friendship when appointed to replace him in Norfolk. He evidently found Northampton a useful ally, for in the year after Somerset's fall Parr was rewarded with the office of Lord Great Chamberlain (resigned by Warwick in his favour), and was subsequently party to the plot which Warwick (then Duke of Northumberland) formed to make Jane Grey Queen on Edward's death. Surviving the failure of this attempt Northampton regained his place at court and died, aged fifty-eight, in 1571.

A number of lords and gentlemen are known to have been with Northampton when he entered Norwich. Among them were Lord Wentworth, Lord Sheffield, Sir Anthony Denny, Sir Ralph Sadler, Sir Richard Lee, Sir Richard Southwell, Sir John Gates, Sir Thomas Paston, Sir Henry Bedingfield, Sir John Suliard, Sir William Walgrave, Sir John Cutts, Sir Thomas Cornwallis, Sir Henry Parker, Sir John Clere, and Sir Ralph Powlet. Not all of these would have come from London: several are Norfolk or Suffolk gentry who probably joined Northampton as he marched through East Anglia. The group includes several prominent political figures, such as Denny, Gates, and Sadler, courtiers such as Sheffield and Southwell, and two experienced soldiers, Wentworth and Lee. The Italian mercenaries were led by one Malatesta. The army was accompanied by a Herald, Gilbert Dethick, Norroy King at Arms.

Of the Norfolk gentry the best known name here is that of Paston. The head of that family in 1549 was old Sir William who had sent the cannon which, having fallen into Kett's hands, now faced the Marquess from Mousehold. Sir Thomas Paston who accompanied Northampton was Sir William's third son, representing the family because his father was too old for battle, his eldest brother was dead, and his second brother probably away at sea. He was brother-in-law to Sheriff Wyndham, whose sister Mary had married Paston's late brother Erasmus. In rather similar case was Sir Henry Parker, who represented the ancient family of Morley which had long held the manor of Hingham. His father, the eighth Lord Morley, was still living but was in his mid sixties. The son seems to have administered the family's affairs in Norfolk and it was presumably against this son, Sir Henry, that the Hingham riots of 1539 had been directed. The Parkers were closely connected with the Boleyns: Sir Henry's second wife Elizabeth was first cousin to Queen Anne, and his sister Jane had married the Queen's brother (George, styled Viscount Rochford) who had shared Anne's fate in 1536. Sir Henry had been knighted at Anne's coronation in 1533 but was not involved in her fall, for we find him a few years later in the party sent to escort the new

Queen Anne of Cleves from Calais. He died shortly after the rebellion, however, in 1553, in the lifetime of his father. In spite of their Boleyn connections the Parkers were staunchly Catholic: Sir Henry's father, the eighth Lord Morley, was an eminent man of letters who took part in Somerset's prosecution in 1550; Sir Henry's son, the ninth Lord, was knighted by Mary but fled the country under her successor on account of his religion.

Another Catholic family of Norfolk was the Bedingfields of Oxborough, represented in Northampton's army by Sir Henry, son of Sir Edmund who was still living. Sir Edmund had early won the favour of Henry VIII and was entrusted by him with the guardianship of Catherine of Aragon, held in Kimbolton Castle while the King was trying to divorce her to marry Anne Boleyn. His son, Sir Henry, was to have a similar charge under Queen Mary when he was appointed Governor of the Tower of London and made custodian of the Princess Elizabeth at Woodstock. Elizabeth graciously forgave him and even visited him at Oxborough in 1578. In 1549, however, Sir Henry was known only as heir to his father. He also was brother-in-law to Sir Edmund Wyndham as they had married sisters, the daughters of Sir Roger Townshend.

Sir John Clere had served on the jury which heard Surrey's case and was a member of the family which owned lands at Ormesby and Stokesby in Norfolk. Sir Thomas Cornwallis, a young man knighted only the year before the rising and still at the beginning of his career, had married into the Catholic family of Jerningham. He was to be a supporter of Mary, in whose reign he was made a Privy Councillor and Comptroller of the Household, but he was deprived of his offices by Elizabeth and spent the rest of his long life on his Suffolk estates.

Paston, Parker, Bedingfield, Cornwallis, and Clere joined Northampton as loyal East Anglian gentlemen. Of these only Cornwallis could really be called a courtier: his father had been Steward of the Household to Prince Edward and his fortune was to be made at court. Several of the other courtiers in Northampton's party also had East Anglian connections. Lord Wentworth held lands in Suffolk and his father, Sir Richard Wentworth, had been Sheriff of Norfolk and Suffolk in 1509 and 1517. Sir Richard Southwell had his seat at Woodrising in Norfolk and had been brought up in the household of the Duke of Norfolk to whom he was distantly related. The Denny family also had Norfolk associations: Sir Anthony's nephew John (Gentleman of the Privy Chamber to Henry VIII) had his seat at Howe, and a grandson Edward was to hold the title Earl of Norwich under Charles I.

The composition of Northampton's force shows that Kett was facing not only a professional army under noble commanders but also a closing of the ranks of the Norfolk gentry. When the rebellion began the gentry of the county were divided by religious and political issues and often separated by large tracts of country. Being also leaderless (after the fall of the Howards) they had been able to take no immediate concerted action. By the time Northampton arrived, however, the local families had evidently forgotten their differences and were united in defence of their county and their class against a common enemy. The underlying solidity of the gentry as a social group is suggested by the close bonds of kinship between many of the local families, bonds which frequently ignored differences of religion and politics. When the seriousness of Kett's rising was recognized the gentry soon united as a family against it, which may be the reason why, after its first weeks, the rebellion did not succeed in gaining footholds in other parts of the county. The local landlords, although caught unprepared, soon took steps to prevent the spread of disorder. Outbreaks in other parts of Norfolk appear to have been promptly confronted and successfully contained by the gentry.

The strength of Northampton's company did not rely on local prestige alone, however, for several of its members were prominent at court or in the King's Council. Thomas Wentworth, who ranked, in this army, immediately after Northampton himself, had considerable experience in both war and diplomacy. He had served under the Duke of Suffolk in France where, in 1523, he had earned his knighthood. Thereafter he joined the household of King Henry's sister Mary and was created baron in 1529. He had supported the King's divorce from Catherine of Aragon, had served on the jury at the trial of Anne Boleyn, and been sent to Calais to receive Anne of Cleves. Like Northampton, Wentworth later backed Warwick against Somerset and was admitted to the Privy Council after the fall of the Protectorate. When he died prematurely two years afterwards he was buried with great honour in Westminster Abbey. His aunt Margery Wentworth had married Sir John Seymour to become mother of the Protector and Queen Jane: Wentworth was therefore first cousin to Somerset and cousin once removed to Edward VI.

Lord Sheffield was probably the youngest of the gentlemen in the company, being only twenty-eight, two years younger than Cornwallis. Like Cornwallis he was at the beginning of what promised to be a successful career at court. He had gained a footing through Thomas Cromwell, in whose household he had been placed, and he managed to survive the fall of his master by impressing the King with his personal qualities. He appears to have been a miniature type of the more famous Earl of Surrey: he was known as a skilled musician, was celebrated in contemporary sonnets, and was at least once imprisoned for unruly conduct. He

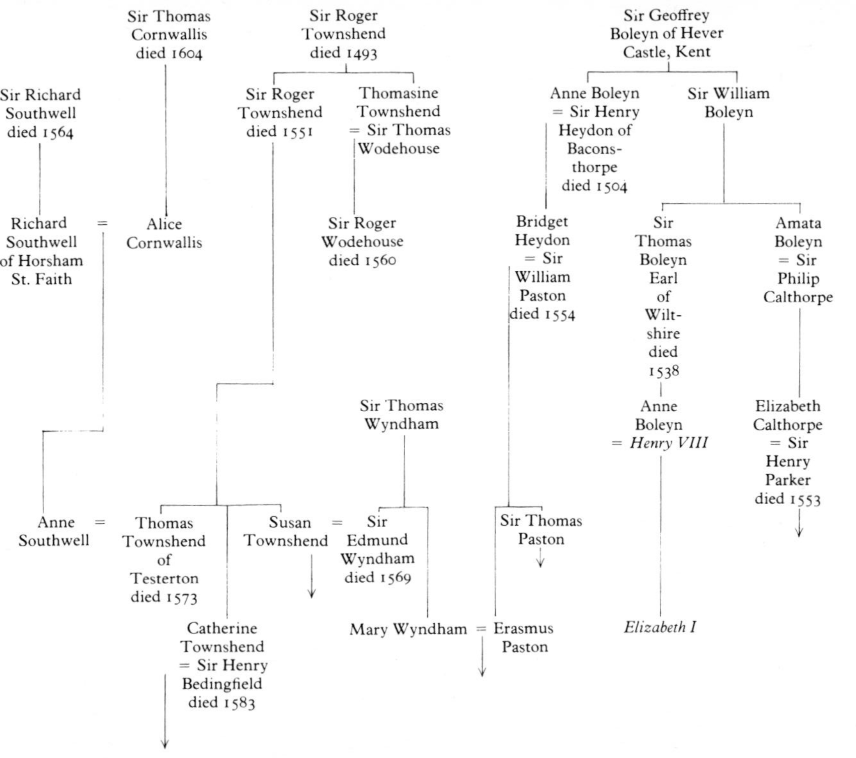

Interrelations among the Norfolk Gentry

was generally admired as an approach to the sixteenth-century ideal of the gentleman courtier, exemplified more grandly by Surrey and, in his younger days, by King Henry himself. Largely on the strength of this popularity he had been created Baron Sheffield of Butterwick at the coronation of Edward VI. Sheffield was the only nobleman to be killed in the Norfolk rising.

A more mundane type of Tudor courtier was Sir Richard Southwell. His uncle and his father had been loyal servants of Henry VII, as Chief Butler and Auditor of the Exchequer respectively. When Richard was orphaned in 1515 the family's local connections secured him a place in the Duke of Norfolk's household and he spent the later years of his boyhood as companion to the young Earl of Surrey. He was Member of Parliament for Norfolk in 1539 and was knighted in 1542. He was the instrument of the court in the trial of his former companion in 1546, for it was Southwell who brought against Surrey the charges which ostensibly caused the fall of the Howards. Henry's will appointed him one of the twelve advisors to the Council of executors. After the rebellion he joined Warwick's party against Somerset but was in the next year imprisoned for his Catholic faith. (The Southwells were strongly attached to the old religion: the jesuit poet and martyr Robert Southwell was a grandson of this Sir Richard.) This taste of persecution stood him in good stead under Mary, but like Bedingfield and Cornwallis he was forced into retirement by the Protestant revival under Elizabeth.

Southwell was evidently an efficient and useful servant of the Crown. Rather similar was Sir Anthony Denny (son of Sir Edmund, a Baron of the Exchequer) who rose to wealth and power in the service of Henry VIII. He received extensive lands after the dissolution and was knighted at Boulogne in 1544. A mark of Henry's confidence was Denny's authorization in 1546 to affix the royal sign manual by means of a stamp to any royal warrant – a measure adopted to relieve the aging King from the pressure of routine business. It was Denny who dared to tell Henry he was dying and to suggest the summoning of Cranmer. Henry's will named him one of the Council of executors. His encounter with the Norfolk rebels was probably his last major undertaking, for he appears to have died later in the year.

Similar professional servants of the Crown were Sir John Gates and Sir Ralph Sadler. Gates had been Gentleman of the Privy Chamber to Henry VII and had continued in the service of Henry VIII. He accompanied the King against the Lincolnshire rebels in 1536 and ten years later he shared with Denny the authority to stamp the royal signature on warrants. In December of 1546 he was sent with Southwell and William Carew to fetch the Duchess of Richmond and Bess Holland from Kenninghall to give evidence at the trial of Norfolk and Surrey. For his part in these proceedings he was rewarded with lands in Essex. He was knighted at the coronation of Edward VI. After the Norfolk rebellion he sided with Warwick and became a Privy Councillor in 1551 and Chancellor of the Duchy of Lancaster in 1552. In the first year of Queen Mary he was executed for complicity in the Jane Grey plot.

Sadler began his career, like Sheffield, in the household of Thomas Cromwell, and subsequently found favour with Henry VIII. By 1540 he was a trusted secretary to the King and had already been on the first of many important diplomatic missions to Scotland. He was knighted in 1542 and sent to Scotland again to arrange a marriage between Prince Edward and the infant Mary Queen of Scots. When war with Scotland broke out Sadler accompanied the army under Hertford, and in 1547, under the same leader (then Lord Protector), distinguished himself at the battle of Pinkie. He was named one of the twelve advisors to the Council by Henry's will. Through Mary's reign he lived in retirement but under Elizabeth he held the confidence of secretary Cecil who sent him on several more diplomatic missions. He died a very wealthy man in 1587.

Sadler had gained considerable military experience in the course of his dealings with the Scots, but the most practised soldier of Northampton's party was surely Sir Richard Lee (or Leigh, or à Lee). Lee had first seen service in Calais in 1533 where he had become involved in fortification and demolition, matters in which he soon became a recognized expert. He was appointed Surveyor of the King's Works in 1540, and in the next year returned to Calais as a member of a commission sent to survey the marches. In 1544 he inspected the fortifications at Tynemouth and was present at the English attacks on Leith and Edinburgh. He was commended by Hertford (the commander in the field), was knighted, and was rewarded with lands in Hertfordshire. For the next three years he was engaged in similar tasks wherever English forts were threatened or hostile forts to be taken. In 1547 he accompanied the Protector's expedition against the Scots and, like Sadler, was present at the battle of Pinkie. He was subsequently employed by both Mary and Elizabeth and died in 1575.

Sadler and Lee were both well-known to Somerset and respected by him for their military skills. They must also have been well-known to each other, having served together in several campaigns. Lee's daughter Anne, moreover, had married Sadler's son Edward, and the grandson Richard eventually inherited Sir Richard's extensive monastic properties.

Although Northampton proved an undistinguished commander

the band of men set against Kett in July included representatives of most major Norfolk families and a number of prominent courtiers, soldiers, and politicians. The expedition failed primarily because the government had been unable at short notice to raise a sufficiently large force. There can be no doubt, however, that by this time Somerset viewed the Norfolk rising as a serious threat, for he sent against it not only the fourth peer of the realm, but also two Privy Councillors (Denny and Southwell), two more peers (Wentworth and Sheffield), a secretary of state (Sadler), and the country's greatest authority on military fortifications (Lee). When we remember how restricted his choice of men was in July of 1549, when his administration was already actively defending itself on so many fronts, the list is impressive indeed.

15. *Northampton's Defeat*

By July 29 Kett knew Northampton was coming. Two days later, a Wednesday, the government forces drew up about a mile outside Norwich and sent forward the Herald, Gilbert Dethick, to summon the city to surrender. The summons made no distinction between the rebels and the citizens: Norwich was confronted by the King's messenger and its occupants, whoever they might be, were required to submit to royal authority. The Herald was answered by Augustine Steward who told him that the Mayor was in the hands of the rebels on Mousehold. Steward could not, or would not, act in this instance without authorization from Codd. Word was accordingly sent to the Mayor, who was evidently sufficiently his own master to receive the message and send reply that the city should surrender. Codd's reply must have been sent with Kett's knowledge, for there is no doubt that Kett could, had he so wished, have prevented, at least for a time, the capitulation of the city. He may have seen that it would be to his strategic advantage to allow Northampton's force to enter Norwich.

Augustine Steward and a number of the citizens then went out and delivered the city sword of state to the Marquess in token of submission. Steward explained Codd's absence and claimed that, although there were many in Norwich who sympathized with Kett, most of the citizens were loyal subjects. The sword was handed to Sir Richard Southwell who, bareheaded, carried it before the Marquess as the government forces entered in procession through St. Stephen's Gate. Kett had withdrawn to Mousehold and Northampton's occupation of the city was unopposed.

Northampton and his officers dined in the council chamber. Then they went into the market place, where a crowd had assembled, to confer with the leaders of the citizens. It was decided that the city should be closed and held against the camp. The decision was unfortunate, for by expending his resources in defence of a sprawling and exposed site Northampton forfeited the little advantage which the training, weapons, and maneuverability of his force might have given him on open ground. His primary objective should have been to disperse the rebels, which would not easily be done by adopting a defensive posture in Norwich. Northampton, however, appointed watches and retired to dine and rest at the house of Augustine Steward.

Towards evening a body of the Italians strayed inexplicably out of the east side of the city and were set upon by a party of Kett's horsemen who tried to encircle them. The Italians managed to regain the city, with the exception of one of their officers who was captured and taken to the heath. The Italians were especially unpopular because they were foreign mercenaries employed against Englishmen, and the unfortunate captive was hanged from the walls of Surrey House. He was hanged, Sotherton says, by one Cayme of Bungay, which may mean that Kett ordered an execution at which Cayme acted as hangman or that Cayme himself was responsible for the decision. The event is notable as the first judicial execution known to have been carried out by the rebels, but it is not clear how the decision was made – whether in the heat of battle or by due process at the Oak of Reformation. The Italians would have been willing to ransom their fellow, and may even have offered to do so.

Perhaps as a result of this careless encounter with the rebels Northampton convened a council of his officers to strengthen the defences. Sir Edward Warner was made Knight-Marshal, and Sir Thomas Paston, Sir John Clere, Sir William Walgrave, Sir Thomas Cornwallis, and Sir Henry Bedingfield were put in command of different parts of the city. The main body of the government forces was camped on the market place, where bonfires were lit to prevent any surprise attack in the dark from Kett's sympathizers in the city. These measures were sensible, given that the city was to be defended, and they proved effective for a time. (Sir Edward Warner of Besthorpe, five miles southwest of Wymondham, who was appointed Knight-Marshal, had been a Member of Parliament, had been a witness against the Earl of Surrey, and had been granted lands in Norfolk by Henry VIII. He was appointed Lieutenant of the Tower in 1552 but was dismissed in the next year. In Mary's reign he suffered for his suspected complicity in Wyatt's rebellion. When Elizabeth succeeded in 1558 he was restored to his office and was returned to Parliament for Norfolk in 1563. Two years later he died and was buried at Plumstead.)

During the night Kett opened fire with his cannon against the city's eastern defences. Little damage, as usual, was achieved by the guns, but the cannonade was only preliminary to a mass assault. The Knight-Marshal aroused the Marquess, who came with some of his officers to the market place to be in readiness. Augustine Steward was sent in search of Wentworth, Denny, Sadler, and Lee, who were evidently lodged in other houses. When all the gentlemen were assembled a council of war was held at which Lee suggested that the western walls be strengthened so that fewer men might hold them and more men, consequently, be freed to meet the attack which would come mostly from the east. The recommendation was eminently sensible and, had it not come too late, might have done something to correct the disadvantage at which Northampton had placed himself by undertaking to defend the city.

When the assault came it was fierce and strong. Many rebels were in the city already and there was fighting in the streets as well as around the perimeter. Kett's men fought desperately and no quarter was given by either side. Yet the defences held and the rebels within the city were unable to disperse Northampton's soldiers. Some three hundred of the insurgents are said to have died in this battle.

By morning the rebels had withdrawn, and while the Marquess breakfasted at the Maid's Head Inn labourers were repairing the damage done to the city gates. Both the soldiers and the citizens had every reason to avoid further conflict with Kett if possible: Northampton's men were considerably outnumbered and the city was suffering serious losses of business and property. All were agreed that an offer of pardon on condition of dispersal should be made to the rebels before risking another general engagement. It was reported that a crowd of them were gathered just outside the Pockthorpe Gate, and accordingly the Herald was sent there accompanied by Augustine Steward and a trumpeter. When he arrived there were no rebels in sight, but a blast on the trumpet soon brought a considerable number down from the heath. The offer of pardon was made but was rejected by one John Flotman of Beccles who was leader of the assembled rebels. Flotman defied Northampton, said that he was a traitor, and asserted that they (the rebels) were loyal subjects and stood in no need of pardon.

Before this parley was concluded, however, there came a general call to arms. The rebels were attacking the Bishopsbridge Gate and had again broken into the meadows between the Cathedral and the Wensum by crossing the river. The Herald's party withdraw the way it had come: through the Pockthorpe Gate and across Whitefriars Bridge. Steward returned to his house in Tombland Alley while the Herald presumably went on to join the commander. Battle had begun again, at about 9 o'clock on Thursday, August 1.

The weakest point in the defences again proved to be the stretch of the eastern perimeter bounded by the river and guarded only by the Bishopsbridge Gate. Again the river was crossed, the gate taken and the street leading from the gate into the city laid open to the rebels. This street, formerly Holmstreet, now Bishopsgate, ran then, as now, a short distance from the bridge in the direction of the Cathedral and then turned northwards around the Cathedral and the Bishop's Palace. It ended in a small square dominated by the church of St. Martin-at-Place (formerly St. Martin-at-Palace or, more fully, St. Martin-at-the-Palace-Gate). On this plain, covering the entrance from Bishopsgate Street, Northampton had placed his guns, and here the fighting was concentrated. Two of the gentlemen, Sir Thomas Cornwallis and Sir Henry Bedingfield, were captured here and one, Lord Sheffield, was killed. Sheffield was fighting in the thick of the battle and was probably taking greater risks than the other defenders felt appropriate. He fought on horseback and, trying to turn his horse, he fell into a ditch and was promptly overcome. He threw off his headgear to show the rebels who he was, expecting they would treat him as a valuable captive and accord him some honour as a peer of the realm, but he was mistaken, for one Fulke, a butcher and carpenter by trade, at once bludgeoned him to death.[1] Fulke was one of those caught and hanged by Warwick after the rebellion. Sheffield was buried with some thirty-five others at St. Martin-at-Place.

Estimates of the casualties of this battle, which lasted until noon, are widely variant. Sotherton, perhaps most reliable, says that no more than forty died altogether, although many more were wounded. Neville claims one hundred and forty rebels slain and a number of the soldiers besides. King Edward notes that Northampton lost one hundred men and that thirty more were taken prisoner. Even if we accept the highest of these figures the loss of life does not seem to have been great considering the number of persons involved. Kett's victory seems to have come rather from demoralising the opposition than from actually destroying it: houses were set afire, the citizens began fleeing through the western gates, several of Northampton's lieutenants were captured, and Lord Sheffield was slain. What seems to have ocurred was not a deliberate withdrawal but an undisciplined general retreat.

There was no pursuit. Northampton managed to collect most of his forces and withdraw with them to Cambridge to await reinforcements. Although he still commanded almost as many men as he had done the day before when he challenged the city to surrender he appears to have made no effort to go back and face the rebels again. It must have been evident to him by this time that the easy surrender of the city had been, in effect if not in intention, a trap to draw him into the labyrinth of streets with its two miles of wall to defend, its nervous citizens to control, and with a considerable body of rebels concealed there ready to emerge at the right moment. Had Northampton now turned back towards Norwich Kett might well have repeated the same maneuvre, withdrawing to Mousehold, allowing the Marquess to enter Norwich, and forcing him to defend it. As long as Kett could keep the government forces on the defensive in the city they could do him no harm and he could damage them at will.

How far the course of events just outlined was due to deliberate strategy on Kett's part is open to question. It is notable, however, that the rebels did attempt to hold the city against Warwick's army three weeks later: if Kett had wished to keep Northampton out of Norwich there was no reason why he should not have defended it on July 31. Another question, which becomes increasingly worrisome as the events of the rebellion unfold, is how far Kett was in control of the rebels' activities. Could he, or any one man, at this time have decided whether the army on Mousehold should defend the city or not? The accounts of this phase of the rebellion show groups and individuals among the rebels acting on their own initiative without reference to Kett, whose own activities during the battles against Northampton are not mentioned. The Herald, for instance, spoke not to Kett but to John Flotman, who appears to have answered on his own authority, and there is also the hanging of the Italian officer, which may have been done without Kett's knowledge. The evidence is inconclusive, however: we do not know that Kett did not authorize the hanging, and Flotman's parley with the Herald can be seen as a diversionary measure to cover the surprise attack which was launched against the Bishopsbridge Gate while negotiations outside the Pockthorpe Gate were still proceeding. We know from certain things which happened after Northampton's retreat that Kett was still at this time an active directive force in the rebellion, but how complete was his control is not certain. Towards the end, in the final battle against Warwick, there is some evidence that Kett no longer led the rebels and that he did not agree with the policies of those who did; but here again the evidence is not conclusive.

Northampton left the city he had foolishly undertaken to defend much worse off than he had found it. Considerable damage was done during the fighting, especially by fire. There seems to have been much more fighting in the streets of Norwich on this Kett's second capture of the city than there had been on the first – presumably because on the first occasion the citizens capitulated soon after the perimeter defences were breached whereas this time Northampton held reserves of professional soldiers at strategic points inside. Many of the citizens who had stayed after the first invasion now fled with Northampton. Kett appears to have established a much stronger presence within the city after the Marquess's defeat – but not before a period of several days of civil disorder and at least some looting had elapsed.

Sotherton describes the aftermath of the fighting on August 1 through the eyes of Augustine Steward. The information he gives must have come from Steward himself and is undoubtedly authentic. After the retreat Steward returned home "doubtful what to do . . . seeing the city empty of all assistance, and every man's door shut." He found his own house empty because his servants had fled with the army. "Comfortless, with a heavy heart," he climbed to the upper storey and looked out at the city. He saw that the rebels "had set all the houses in the street called Holmstreet afire on both sides, with a great part of the Hospital, houses of office that belonged to the poor in that house, and also the city gates called Bishops gates with the lead thereof molten and the gates and houses of them of Pockthorpe, Magdalene, St. Austins, Conisford, and Bearstreet all on fire that day." (Sotherton is romancing a little: Steward cannot have seen all this from the top of his house.)

Presently there appeared "a great number of rebels, with a drum before them, who came to his house, and rapped, and cried, 'Set fire in the gates.' And he being greatly afraid (for all his servants were fled from him), himself alone unshut the gates; whom presently they took, and plucked off his gown (which he used at that time), calling him a rebel, and threatening him a most shameful death." They were looking for Northampton, whom they knew had lodged with Steward, and they searched the house thoroughly in spite of the alderman's protestations that Northampton had left the city. Eventually, when they were satisfied that the Marquess was not in the house, Steward gave them money to go away, but "there came another company that brake open his shop and in burdens carried away whatever was therein, till one Doo of their company, a servant of Mr. Smith of Huntingfield, had sharply told them for robbing and spoiling they should all be hanged, whereupon many of their fardles were cast again into the shop: whom to rid was fain to be cut both shirt cloths and doublet cloths of fustian, and given them to save the rest: and after their departure came another company to have spoiled, had not the said Doo and three or four more kept them off, saying he was spoiled before."

From the ravages of fire which, in the absence of any organization to combat it, might have been serious the city was saved by a heavy shower of rain. Looting and terrorization, however, continued for several days, directed especially against the wealthy citizens who, like Steward, had cooperated conspicuously with Northampton. Many of these men took flight, hiding their wealth and valuables in places where they hoped the rebels would not find them. A little later, when order was restored, Kett declared all those who had fled the city traitors and enemies of the King, the argument being that he himself represented the King's best interests and that those who opposed him or banded with his enemies were therefore traitors. Northampton was the arch-traitor and the citizens who fled with him were his abettors. The goods of these citizens were declared confiscate, but the order does not seem to have been systematically carried out, for Sotherton tells that many servants were able to preserve the bulk of their masters' goods by baking and roasting foods for the rebels from their masters' houses. Some of the citizens who remained hid themselves "in false roofs, and other secret places" for fear of being taken prisoner, as many were, by the rebels.

"The state of the city began to be in most miserable case, so that all men looked for utter destruction, both of life and goods. Then the remnant that feared God, seeing the plague thus of sorrow increasing, fell to prayer and holy life, and wished but to see the day that after they might talk thereover, hoping [i.e. expecting] never to recover help again, nor to see their city prosper" (Sotherton). Even the churches were not safe, for the rebels used them freely as shelter against the weather, and acts of desecration were committed.

Kett set up a garrison camp in the Cathedral grounds and began, in the same way as he had done on Mousehold, to establish a rough duplicate of the administration he had overthrown. He appointed aldermen and constables for the city from his own men, and gave them authority to conscript citizens to serve as watchmen. He also ordered his own people to guard the strategic points and public buildings, in particular the city gates, the castle, and the guildhall. (The two latter housed the jails of the county and the city respectively, both used by Kett to confine his prisoners.) Steward was obliged to help in organizing the citizens' watch. He endeavoured to maintain morale among them, and even attempted a little spiritual propaganda among the rebels in hopes of weakening their determination. He arranged for Dr. Barrett and other preachers to address Kett's men – "which, notwithstanding, helped not at all, for so impudent were they and out of order that no one could restrain them" (Sotherton).

16. *Attempts to Spread the Rebellion*

By the time of Northampton's defeat Kett's army had been encamped on Mousehold for three weeks. It was quite clear by then, and had been since the York Herald's visit on July 21, that the government did not see Kett as an ally in the extirpation of local corruption but treated him as a rebel. There were only two courses open therefore: Kett could either come to terms with the government (which would mean disbanding and accepting a pardon, having achieved nothing and running the risk that the pardon might not be honoured), or he could refuse terms and expect a military confrontation. The government would make no compromise with Kett, and the rebels, after their two victories, first over the city and then over Northampton, would have been in no mind to consider surrender. Another military confrontation was therefore inevitable. The government would go on sending forces against Kett as long as he held his ground.

Theoretically Kett, committed to maintain the rebellion, could choose between defensive and offensive courses of action. He could either establish his own administration in a particular area and hope to defend this area against all government efforts to reclaim it, or he could attempt to overthrow the government itself. But the Norfolk rising was very much a local matter and there is no evidence that the rebels at any time contemplated any direct coercion of the national government. Their aim was to enforce the desired reforms in the areas they could control, hoping at first for government backing and, when this was not forthcoming, endeavouring to maintain their local administration against the government's efforts to drive them out.

But if Kett was to maintain local control he would need to hold a far larger area than that of Norwich and Mousehold. As long as his effective power was limited to a single city and a single garrison it would be only a matter of time before the government found sufficient forces to encircle and overpower him. To hold his ground Kett would need to govern at least several other large towns which might be garrisoned if necessary and a large stretch of country to give him provision and room to maneuvre. Kett did in fact exercise great influence over the countryside for some fifteen or twenty miles around Norwich, but this was of little use to him, except as a source for provisions, as long as Norwich was his only base, for the government forces, when they came, would easily be able to find him and to force a confrontation on their own terms. Kett had Mousehold, but he had no reserves, nowhere else to withdraw to, no way of outmaneuvering his opponents.

In the weeks between Northampton's defeat and Warwick's arrival Kett made several attempts to improve his position by expanding his territory, and in the climate of widespread discontent that prevailed in the summer of 1549 there seemed a real possibility that he might achieve this. Towards the end of July a camp was formed near Castle Rising by country people from the regions around Downham Market, Swaffham, and King's Lynn. It is likely, although no details are known, that this camp was inspired by Mousehold and may even have been directed by Kett's agents. The establishment of a camp near Castle Rising suggests that the plan was to take Lynn in much the same way as Kett had taken Norwich. The capture of Lynn would have been a substantial advantage for the rebels, but there in western Norfolk the gentry were ready and organized and were able to dislodge the insurgents from the camp. The people were not dispersed, however, and withdrew about twenty-five miles southeastwards to Watton, from which place they established control over the points at which the Little Ouse river could be crossed in the region of Thetford.

Because this force arrived at Watton a little before Northampton's approach and left a little after his withdrawal it is most likely that the rebels planned some kind of strategic action coordinate with Kett's defence at Norwich. Possibly they hoped to hinder the Marquess's advance, or to attack him from behind once he had passed, or simply to cut off his retreat – but nothing of the kind seems to have been accomplished. It can hardly be accidental, however, that the rebels driven from the region of King's Lynn journeyed twenty-five miles southeastwards to a point so close to the line of Northampton's march from Cambridge to Norwich. Early in August they abandoned Watton and many of their number joined Kett on Mousehold. Decisive evidence is again lacking, but there are indications here of an attempt to expand the Norwich rebellion into western Norfolk and to bring two rebel forces, some thirty miles apart, into concerted action for the defence of the county against the government.

At about the same time, in late July, a rebel camp was formed at Hingham. There would be little point in making a separate camp only fifteen miles from Norwich unless some strategy was planned. A spontaneous rising at Hingham (where there had been riots for ten years before) would surely have united immediately with Kett on Mousehold instead of maintaining a separate, weak, and exposed outpost in a small village. Hingham is roughly mid way between Norwich and Watton, and like Watton it lies a few miles to the north of the road which troops from London would take to reach the county town. There may have been a plan for coordinated action between the camps at Watton, Hingham, and Mousehold to hinder the approach of Northampton's army. (It may not be coincidence that Hingham was the domain of Sir Henry Parker who was with the government forces.)

What the rebels of Hingham intended was not discovered because their camp was attacked by a local force under Sir Edmund Knyvett of Buckenham Castle. The dates of these actions are not recorded, but this would probably have been shortly before Northampton's arrival. The issue of the battle was uncertain: the rebels appear to have held their ground but Knyvett withdrew in good order with his retainers and returned unscathed to his fortress. What happened next shows that the Hingham camp acknowledged Kett's authority: the events at Hingham were reported to Kett with the suggestion that reprisal should be taken against Knyvett, but Kett felt that the castle was too strong and too far (some twelve miles) from Mousehold, and no action was taken. The camp at Hingham may have been maintained after this, but it is unlikely. Knyvett obviously posed a serious threat to its safety and Kett had admitted that Knyvett could not, for the moment, be stopped. Under these circumstances the Hingham rebels would have been wise to join (or rejoin) the camp at Mousehold. At any rate, no more is heard of the camp at Hingham.

The action at Castle Rising and Knyvett's expedition against Hingham show that by the end of July the Norfolk gentry were beginning to initiate organized local measures against the rebellion. The Wymondham rising had caught them unprepared, and the camp at Mousehold was now far too big for them to tackle without government forces to back them, but their actions just recited were decisive in preventing the rebellion from taking root in other centres in the county. As long as Kett could be contained on Mousehold he was as good as beaten, even although he held Norwich and made prisoners of the surrounding gentry in the meantime.

Sir Edmund Knyvett stands out as unusually heroic among his fellows. He had, however, the advantage of being in the right place with a defensible fortress, an advantage possessed by few of the other Norfolk gentry. The Knyvetts had been long established in Norfolk. Sir Edmund's great-great-great-grandfather had married the heiress of Sir John Clifton, the benefactor of Wymondham Abbey, and in this way the family came into possession of the twelfth-century castle at New Buckenham. Other advantageous

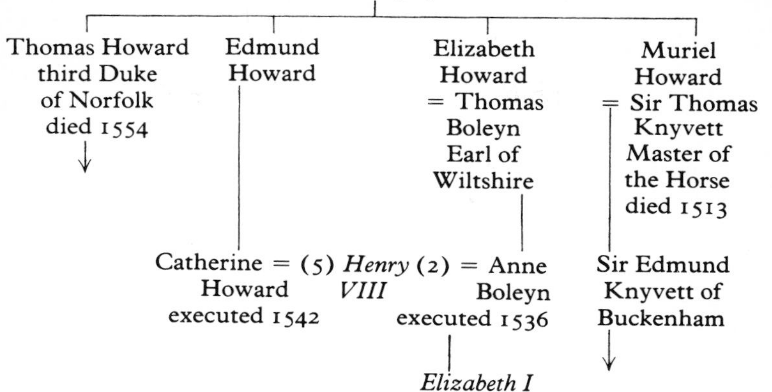

marriages were made by later generations, connecting the Knyvetts with some of the most powerful baronial families. Sir Edmund's great-grandfather married a daughter of Humphrey Stafford, Duke of Buckingham, who was himself descended from Edward III. Sir Edmund's uncle (another Sir Edmund, who died in 1546) married the eventual heiress of the barony of Berners and of the manor of Ashwellthorpe three miles southeast of Wymondham. Sir Edmund's mother had been a Howard, daughter of the second Duke of Norfolk, and Sir Edmund himself was therefore cousin to two of Henry's queens and cousin once removed to the Princess Elizabeth. Knyvett later joined Warwick's army and played a significant part in the final battle against the rebels.

The rebel camps at Castle Rising, Watton, and Hingham remain mysterious because the nature of their connection with Kett's revolt cannot be determined. These other risings might have been part of a plan emanating from Mousehold and intending to win the whole of Norfolk for the rebel cause, or they might have been spontaneous risings prompted only by Kett's example. Clear evidence of Kett's active desire to expand his territory in the early days of August comes from his dealings with Yarmouth, an important town and sea-port less than twenty miles east of Norwich.

In the early days of the rising a contingent from the region of Bungay and Beccles, just across the Suffolk border, had marched against Yarmouth and captured John Millicent and Nicholas Fenn, the town bailiffs. The townspeople nonetheless refused to admit the rebels and the captives somehow regained their freedom. The attempt had failed and most of the men involved joined Kett on Mousehold. Vice-Admiral Sir Thomas Wodehouse, who was patrolling the east coast, was able to report to Somerset that Yarmouth was loyal, and in a letter of July 26 the Protector congratulated the bailiffs and warned the town to be on its guard.

Kett could not forget Yarmouth. It was the second town of Norfolk, centre of a major fishing industry, and lay only twenty miles away – in his rear, as it were, when he faced government forces coming from the west. If the rebellion was to maintain itself Yarmouth would have to be soon brought under control. On August 5, as soon as order had been restored in Norwich after Northampton's withdrawal, Kett turned his attention to the problem. He dispatched Nicholas Byron with one hundred men to take the town. Byron carried this commission, signed by Kett and Aldrich:

> Be it known to all men, that we Robert Kett and Thomas Aldrich, commissioners of the King's Camp at Mousehold, have appointed out of our camp aforesaid, one hundred of men to return from us to Yarmouth, for the maintenance of the King's town there against our enemies.
>
> Also we do certify you, that we, for the more sufficient and necessary victualling of our said one hundred men, do appoint Richard Smith, Thomas Clarke, and John Rotherham, and also to take up horses for the further aiding of our said men.
>
> Dated at the King's Great Camp at Mousehold the 5th day of August in the 3rd year of the reign of our Sovereign Lord King Edward the Sixth.[1]

The hundred men were only a token force in case the town should comply with the order. In the event Yarmouth refused and Byron presumably returned with his men to Mousehold.

This could hardly be the end of the matter. The townspeople, anticipating more serious trouble, at once sent three burgesses, George Millicent, Gilbert Grice, and John Echard, to report to the King's Council. Somerset wrote in reply, on August 6, that he himself would be bringing an army into Norfolk to settle the rebellion, as at that time, after first hearing of Northampton's defeat, he planned to do. But it took Somerset time to get his army together and before he was ready Kett made an attempt to take Yarmouth by force.

On August 17 a large body of men from Mousehold arrived at the walls of the town. They had procured cannon from nearby Lowestoft and duly opened fire. They were repulsed and withdrew about a mile southwards along the coast to regroup in

Gorleston. Meanwhile the townsmen devised a strategem. A large stack of hay stood somewhere between the rebels and the town walls. To this the townsmen set fire, and the strong north wind fanned the flames and drove the smoke into the faces of the rebels. Under this cover a party of men from the town made a surprise attack, capturing some thirty of the rebels as well as six cannon which were taken into the town. The men from Mousehold were now thoroughly angry and seem to have abandoned strategy in an effort to do as much damage to Yarmouth as possible. They destroyed much of the material designed for reconstruction of the harbour, which had been left outside the walls. They then crossed the Yare and approached the south gates of the town, to which they did some damage before being driven off by the guns from the walls. At this they retreated and no further attempts on Yarmouth were made.

Kett's failure to spread the rebellion was most serious. In spite of the elation at the victory over Northampton it must have been obvious that unless the rising could spread and grow quickly and strongly its days were numbered. Kett tried desperately to achieve this growth in the early days of August, and had his plans succeeded he might have held, besides Norwich, the important towns of Yarmouth and King's Lynn at opposite ends of the county, and the whole of Norfolk might then have been brought under his control. It would then have been very difficult to dislodge him if, with a degree of popular support, he had been able to employ something like guerrilla tactics against the government forces. In fact all his efforts came to nothing in spite of the favourable atmosphere created by his victory over the Lord Lieutenant. He failed because of the resistance of the citizens and gentry who had been caught off guard by the phenomenal march on Norwich but whose organization and resolution had improved in the meantime. It may also have been that the initial promise of Kett's rapid recruitment had not been fulfilled: perhaps most of those who would join him had done so in the first few days, leaving little support for later efforts to expand the rebellion.

17. *Warwick's Army*

The King's Council met on August 3 to discuss the news of Northampton's defeat. This was perhaps their darkest hour of that troubled summer, for besides Kett's victory in Norfolk they were faced with a large rebel army in the west still besieging Exeter and with an imminent declaration of war from France. It was inevitably decided that a stronger force must be sent into Norfolk as soon as possible, and the orders for assembling such a force were issued at once. Somerset himself was to lead the expedition.

A week later, on August 10, the Protector's intention to command the Norfolk army was publicly announced. Very soon afterwards, however, Somerset changed his mind and gave the command to the Earl of Warwick. The decision was fateful, for Warwick's victory over Kett, his success in putting down the rebellion which Somerset's policies had raised, and the army which he controlled in order to do so, gave him the power, shortly after his return from Norfolk, to overthrow the Protectorate. If Somerset himself had led the army against Kett he would surely have won – his military reputation and experience were certainly no less than Warwick's – and he would probably thereby have satisfied the Council, at least for a time, that his lenience in domestic matters did not include the tolerance of civil disorder. Presumably the news of the relief of Exeter determined the Protector to send Warwick to Norfolk instead of to the west or to the north as had been planned. Russell was evidently gaining control of the western situation, thus releasing Warwick for service in Norfolk and allowing Somerset to remain at the seat of government in the capital.

Pollard suggests that Somerset could not himself lead an army against Kett "without alienating the popular support which his domestic policy had brought him,"[1] but this does not explain why the Duke for a week or more held the intention of leading the army. It would, besides, have been naive of Somerset to suppose that the people would dissociate the Protector from the actions of the officers he commissioned. Such motives of policy are unlikely to have affected Somerset's decision: had he been feeling particularly insecure in August he would surely have put himself in charge of an army instead of leaving himself virtually defenceless.

Warwick was on his way northwards when he received his orders. On July 22 it had been decided that he should be sent with reinforcements for Russell into the west, but by July 28 Somerset had wisely seen that Herbert, who had considerable influence in the west country, was the proper man to support Russell and that Warwick, whose interests were largely in the northern and midland counties, should go north. By August 10 the Earl had reached Warwick castle, where he wrote to secretary William Cecil a letter which is puzzling because it appears to acknowledge his appointment as commander of the Norfolk army. On the same day Somerset published his intention to take command himself, which means either that there is some error in the dating of Warwick's letter or that Warwick had been appointed to join the army but not yet told he was to command it. (The letter will bear this latter interpretation.) Warwick's letter is mostly concerned, however, with the Marquess of Northampton whom Warwick thought should be given a chance to redeem the disgrace of his initial failure at Norwich. After thanking the Protector for his appointment to the army the Earl continues: "I do think myself bounden to my Lord's grace and the council for enabling me to receive so great a charge, so I cannot but wish that it might please the same to permit and suffer my Lord Marquess of Northampton to continue still in the force of his commission." If the Marquess is excluded from the new army, Warwick argues, "having lately by misfortune received discomfort enough, haply this might give him occasion to think himself utterly discredited, and so for ever discourage him." The Earl even offers to serve under Northampton if the Council should see fit to reappoint him.[2] Northampton was already alienated from Somerset by the difficulties created over his divorce and by his marginal complicity in the criminal doings of the Protector's brother Thomas who had been executed only five months before. Warwick saw that if Northampton were excluded from a share in the final victory over Kett he would be disgraced and would become hostile, and possibly dangerous, to the administration. There are no grounds for reading ulterior motives into Warwick's diplomacy at this point, but the outcome was favourable to his cause in the quarrel which developed between himself and the Protector, for in taking Northampton as his colleague to Norwich he preserved the goodwill of that nobleman and later enjoyed his support.[3]

The following proclamation was issued on August 15:

> The King's Majesty, by the advice of his most entirely beloved uncle the Lord Protector, and the rest of his highness' council, straightly chargeth and commandeth all gentlemen, of what estate, degree, or condition soever they be, who hath their

habitation and dwelling in Essex, to depart from the court and the city of London and other places near unto them into their several habitations in the said county of Essex with all convenient speed, there to remain till they shall know further of the King's majesty's pleasure; likewise all such gentlemen as hath their habitations and dwellings in Suffolk, to depart unto their said habitations in Suffolk and there to remain until such time as they shall have commandment from the King's majesty or from the Earl of Warwick; and further that all gentlemen inhabitants of Norfolk do repair to the said Earl of Warwick so that they be with the said Earl to attend upon him in the King's majesty's army in his conduct and leading, for his highness' better service, upon Saturday next following [August 17], or Sunday at the furthest. And this, his said majesty, by the advice aforesaid, most straightly chargeth all persons to whom it may appertain, to follow and execute with all convenient speed and diligence, upon pain of his highness' indignation and displeasure.[4]

By August 15 it had been decided that Warwick should lead the army which was by this time more or less assembled, except for the local gentry and their retainers who are instructed in the proclamation to make ready. The numbers of the forces involved are variously given: Sotherton estimates Warwick's army at 12,000, Neville at 14,000, and King Edward, who is most likely to be accurate because in this case he would have the best informed sources, gives 6,000 footsoldiers and 1,500 horsemen. Warwick probably set out on August 20 and, proceeding by the usual route – Cambridge, Newmarket, Thetford, Wymondham – he reached Norwich on August 24.

At Cambridge he was joined by Northampton, who had probably kept with him some of the soldiers and a number of the gentlemen who had fled with him from Norwich. All of these would now have placed themselves under Warwick's command. At same time a band of fugitive citizens from Norwich presented themselves and asked pardon for any complicity unwillingly incurred in the rebellion. Warwick acknowledged they were not criminally at fault, but also suggested that Norwich might have made a firmer stand against the rebels in the early days of the rising. The citizens received the King's pardon and were told to accompany the army back to Norwich.

Warwick arrived in Wymondham on August 22, having been joined by Lord Willoughby's force and a number of Norfolk gentry on his way through the county. By this time his party included, besides himself and Northampton, the following notable persons: Lord Willoughby of Parham, Lord Grey of Powis, Lord Bray, Warwick's sons Ambrose and Robert Dudley, Henry

Willoughby, Sir Thomas Gresham, Sir Marmaduke Constable, William Devereux, Sir Edmund Knyvett, Sir Thomas Palmer, and Sir Andrew Flammock. The army had among its officers five peers of the realm, three sons of peers, and several experienced soldiers and administrators.

Warwick himself is something of an enigma because of his subsequent actions in overthrowing the Protectorate and in attempting to divert the Tudor succession to his daughter-in-law Jane Grey, actions which (because they ended in failure) at once caused him, rather like Richard III, to be labelled as one of our history's villains. Because his career ended in the plot to gain control of the throne Warwick's earlier activities have been interpreted as moves directed towards this end: it is usually suggested that Warwick overthrew Somerset to gain power for himself and, in the same way, that he saw his command of the Norfolk army as a means to overthrow the Duke. But there is no evidence that Warwick was a patient plotter of this kind. On the contrary, it seems that he turned against Somerset only because, like most of his colleagues on the Council, he felt that the summer of 1549 had demonstrated the failure of the Protector's policies. The evidence suggests that he did not decide to act against Somerset until some time after his departure for Norwich, for Warwick and Somerset appear to have maintained mutual confidence at least into July of 1549, and there are no indications of hostility from Warwick towards the Protector until after the defeat of Kett.[5]

Born John Dudley probably about 1504, Warwick was son of Edmund Dudley who had been executed in 1510 on the accession of Henry VIII for his over-zealous pursuit of the grasping financial policies of Henry VII. The sentence was largely a matter of political expediency whereby the new King could seem to disapprove of the abuses of the previous reign while inheriting their fruits. John Dudley was young enough to be unimplicated in his father's fall, and on the strength of his connections was able to gain a footing at court when he came of age. From the first he excelled as a soldier. Like Somerset Warwick won his knighthood in Suffolk's expedition to France in 1523, and thereafter he and Edward Seymour were frequently together in the King's service, becoming close friends and allies. Dudley won favour at court in the next decade, served in the suppression of the Pilgrimage of Grace, and was created Viscount Lisle in 1542. He served against the Scots in the wars of 1542–1543, was made a Privy Councillor, and in 1543 became Lord High Admiral. In the later years of Henry VIII he was sent on several military and diplomatic missions to Scotland and to France, often acting in close cooperation with the Earl of Hertford. On Henry's death he was, after Hertford, the most powerful lord in England. The new coronation honours elevated him to the earldom of Warwick and to the office of Lord Great Chamberlain. (He succeeded Hertford as Chamberlain and resigned the office of Lord High Admiral in favour of Thomas, Lord Seymour of Sudeley, Hertford's brother.) He accompanied Somerset against the Scots in 1547 and distinguished himself in action at the battle of Pinkie. Throughout the first two years of the Protectorate he appears to have supported Somerset and to have raised no serious obstruction or dissent. There is evidence that, like many of his fellow councillors, he disagreed with Somerset's policy on enclosures in 1548, but this can hardly have been a deep division between them at first since it occasioned no change in their personal relationship and resulted in no action until the autumn of 1549.[6]

The man who confronted Kett in August was in many ways the second figure in England: his reputation as a soldier was rivalled only by that of Somerset and in terms of power and wealth none but the Protector stood above him. (As a recently created earl he was outranked by several, but in the higher reaches of Tudor politics rank could count for much less than nearness to the Crown – witness the great influence wielded at different times by untitled men such as Thomas Cromwell and William Cecil.) There can be no doubt that he was the ideal man for the task: once Somerset had decided not to go himself to Norfolk Warwick was the inevitable choice. It is a mark of the national seriousness of Kett's rebellion that Warwick was sent to quell it.

The rest of Warwick's story can be briefly told. After the fall of Somerset in October, 1549, he became the leader of the Council. For a while he and Somerset remained on good terms. The Duke returned to his seat on the Council after a few weeks, and in June of the next year Warwick's eldest son married Somerset's daughter Anne. In October, 1551, Warwick was created Duke of Northumberland. Three months later Somerset was executed for treasonable activities in which he had become involved since his fall from power. As the health of the King began to fail in 1553 Northumberland desperately sought some means of preventing the succession of the next Tudor heir, Mary, an avowed Catholic, who would reverse most of the domestic and foreign policies of her brother and her father. The only acceptable dynastic alternative was the line of the late Princess Mary, daughter of Henry VII, from whose descendants was selected the Lady Jane Grey. In May, 1553, Jane Grey was married to Northumberland's son Guildford Dudley. When Edward VI died in July Northumberland proclaimed Jane Queen, but he was quite easily outmanoeuvred by Mary to whom he soon surrendered. He was executed shortly afterwards.

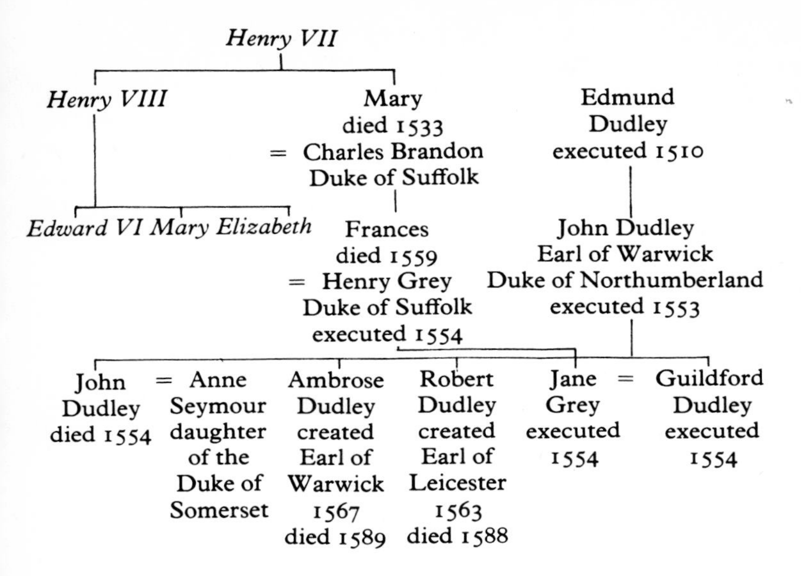

With him in the Norfolk army were two of his younger sons, Ambrose and Robert, both later implicated in his fall but pardoned on account of their youth. Ambrose was probably about twenty-one in 1549 and Robert some three or four years younger. Both were to win favour under Elizabeth. Ambrose became a courtier, soldier, and scholar of the Elizabethan court and died honourably of wounds received in his country's service. Robert became the celebrated Earl of Leicester who was for many years the Queen's favourite and who came close to being her husband. Both were relatively inexperienced in 1549 and were with the army only because their father was its commander.

Besides Warwick and Northampton three peers are known to have accompanied the army: Edward, third Baron Grey of Powis, John, second Baron Bray, and William, first Baron Willoughby of Parham. Bray and Grey of Powis were figures of little political importance who had inherited their titles from more distinguished ancestors. Willoughby, on the other hand, was a soldier of some distinction who had been ennobled for his own merits on the accession of Edward VI. He was a young man in 1549, whose career was still in its early stages. His vigorous action in the Norfolk campaign was rewarded in the later years of Edward's reign with the Chief Stewardship of the Duchy of Calais, but in spite of so promising a beginning Willoughby never rose to the first ranks of power.

Henry Willoughby was of a different branch of the family, being one of the Willoughbys of Wollaton in Nottinghamshire and of Middleton in Warwickshire. He was son of Sir Edward Willoughby and father of Francis Willoughby of Wollaton, and is one of the few gentlemen known to have been killed in battle against Kett. He is probably the same "Henry Wilby of Middleton Hall" whose burial Blomefield found recorded in the register of St. Simon's and St. Jude's church in Norwich. Three other gentlemen who died in the fighting were also buried here: Giles Foster and Thomas Lynsye, both of Warwickshire, and one Lucie (or Lusonn) of Northamptonshire.[7]

Sir Thomas Gresham accompanied the second army against Kett, and his house, Intwood Hall, some three miles southwest of Norwich, served as Warwick's headquarters on the night of August 23. Gresham, whose family came from the Norfolk village of that name, was son to Sir Richard Gresham, a former Lord Mayor of London who died in the year of the rising, and nephew to Sir John, a prosperous London merchant. In 1549 he was in his thirtieth year, beginning a brilliant career as financial adviser to the government. He is best remembered as the founder of the Royal Exchange. It was, of course, his Norfolk properties and connections, not his financial abilities, which placed him in Warwick's company on this occasion. Gresham had married a widow, Anne Rede, who was sister-in-law to Augustine Steward, and he was to become (through the marriage of his illegitimate daughter) father-in-law to Sir Nathaniel Bacon, the brother of Lord Chancellor Francis Bacon.

Sir Thomas Palmer was an experienced soldier and military engineer. He had begun his career as Gentleman Usher to Henry VIII, had seen service in France, and was knighted at Calais in 1532. In the Protector's Scottish war he had assisted at the seige of Haddington as commander of the external English forces. He was, however, captured on this occasion by the Scottish besiegers, for which Somerset greatly blamed him. Palmer felt he had acted only in accord with his orders and thereafter felt some resentment against the Protector. He was an old colleague and friend of the Earl of Warwick. He supported Warwick in the overthrow of the Protectorate, and in 1551 Palmer was the first to voice the charge of treason against Somerset. His association with Warwick brought him into trouble on the accession of Mary, however, for like Sir John Gates he was executed for complicity in the affair of Jane Grey.

The other gentlemen of the party can be dealt with briefly. Sir Marmaduke Constable was a member of the family of Constable of Flamborough which had provided leadership for the Pilgrimage of Grace in 1536. Sir Andrew Flammock was a friend and dependant of Warwick's. William Devereux was younger son of Walter Devereux, first Viscount Hereford, and was therefore great-uncle to Robert, second Earl of Essex, the favourite of Queen Elizabeth who was executed in 1600.

18. *Warwick's Victory*

At Wymondham on August 22 Warwick paused to receive local reinforcements and then proceeded on the next day only some six miles to Sir Thomas Gresham's house at Intwood. On the morning of August 24 he sent the Norroy Herald, Gilbert Dethick, to order the city to receive his army. As the Herald approached St. Stephen's Gate news of his coming was brought to Kett, who appears to have been in the city at the time. Kett ordered Augustine Steward, the Deputy Mayor, and Robert Rugge, a former Mayor and brother to the Bishop, to go out to meet the Herald. Steward and Rugge were chosen because they both represented the lawfully constituted authorities of the city, but why Kett wished to allow these authorities to negotiate independently with Warwick, when he could have met the Herald himself or have barred the city gates, is something of a mystery. It might be taken as a sign that Kett did not rule out the possibility of surrender to Warwick on suitable terms.

Steward and Rugge suggested to the Herald that the offer of pardon on condition of surrender be repeated to the rebels. Kett must have known that they would say this, and would not have permitted them to make the suggestion unless surrender on suitable terms appeared to him a real possibility. The Herald duly returned to Warwick, who agreed that the pardon should again be offered. Both sides seem to have wished to avoid bloodshed. Warwick was almost certainly outnumbered by the rebels, perhaps in a ratio approaching two to one, and they occupied the better ground. The Earl's victory in event of battle was by no means certain. Kett, having failed to spread the rebellion beyond Norwich, probably realized that nothing in the long run would be achieved by another military victory. The government evidently regarded him as a rebel and, unless he could hope to overthrow the government itself, his best course would be to make what terms he could. When the Herald returned with a trumpeter he was readmitted on Kett's authority and taken by some forty of the rebels, along with Steward and Rugge, through the city to the Bishopsgate bridge. There, when a large crowd had been summoned from the camp by the trumpeter, Dethick was permitted to read his message.

The crowd, which according to Sotherton stretched over a quarter of a mile, seemed good humoured and greeted the Herald with shouts of "God save the King!" When silence fell the Herald delivered a somewhat undiplomatic speech accusing the rebels of treason and other crimes and warning them that unless they accepted this last offer of mercy they would be forcibly put down by Warwick's army. Some were indeed intimidated by these words, but most were angered. The Herald himself was called a traitor. Some said the offered pardon was a deception and would not be honoured. Others said that the Herald was not really a King's messenger but an agent of the local gentry hired to mislead them. His gorgeous coat, they said, was not the genuine Herald's garb but a costume made up of old church vestments: the gentry, they said, had "put on him a piece of an old cape for his coat of armour." The situation resembled that which Parker's bold sermon had created a month before. Threats were heard among the crowd against the Herald and his supporters.

At this point Kett arrived and escorted the Herald to another part of the field where the message could be read to another section of the crowd. Why did Kett not receive the Herald in the first place? If he was indeed willing to hear the terms of the surrender why did he not arrive sooner? The answer may lie in a matter of protocol. The Herald probably had instructions to read his message to the people at large and to give Kett no marks of special recognition. If Kett wished to hear the terms in person he would therefore have to stand by as they were read to the crowd. As leader, however, he would wish to preserve some token of his status. By arriving late on the scene he was able to do this, to meet the Herald at a disadvantage and, by acting as his rescuer, make his own authority evident. The Herald had been given a frightening taste of the rebels' hostile power, had been obliged to accept tacitly Kett's protection, and was now to deliver the message a second time in Kett's presence. It is not impossible that Kett's agents staged this whole sequence of events.

What happened next, however, was unforeseen, and put an end to the balance of negotiation which had been initiated. As the Herald was making his speech for the second time a boy in the crowd made an insulting gesture, exposing his buttocks before the Herald's face, and a soldier from Warwick's army, who had strayed across out of curiosity, was so incensed at this that he shot and killed the boy with an arrow. This broke the rebels' discipline which, up to this point, appears to have been generally maintained. The crowd became angry again, raising the cry of treachery, and a party of horsemen rode off to the heath to spread the alarm and to prepare for attack. The Herald moved towards the city and Kett, trying to salvage the negotiations, went with him.

Kett was considering the Herald's suggestion that he should come in person to discuss terms with Warwick under a truce. One of the matters to be clarified was that of Kett's own pardon and of the pardons of his brother and other rebel leaders. It is likely (as Sotherton affirms) that the Ketts were explicitly excluded from the pardon offered by the Herald, but it is quite possible that had Kett and Warwick been able to meet for discussion a general and satisfactory offer of pardon might have been made. There is much to indicate that Kett favoured the Herald's suggestion, but the moment was not propitious. His forces were no longer under his control: even had he been able to leave the field it would have been obvious to Warwick that Kett was not in a position to speak for the camp.

The matter was decided by a band of rebels on horseback who, seeing their leader moving after the Herald, rode to intercept him saying (according to Sotherton), "Whither away, whither away, Mr. Kett? If you go we will go with you, and with you will live and die." The words may be taken as a straightforward affirmation of loyalty, but in the context of events what was said can also be seen as an assertion that Kett would not be allowed to go before Warwick as the sole representative of the rebel cause. It may have been that Kett was hoping to negotiate a surrender, that other leaders among the rebels disapproved of this, and were intervening to prevent Kett from gaining terms which might have resulted in a general surrender. The mood of the camp, in contrast to that of Kett himself at this point, seems to have been distinctly belligerent. Kett remained with his men, the negotiations were at an end, and the Herald reported to Warwick that the final offer of pardon had met with no response.

Warwick now brought up his army to face the southwestern walls of the city. The gates were closed and the defences manned by the rebels. Before the fighting began Codd and Aldrich were somehow able to escape from Norwich and join Warwick. Their being let out suggests a certain confusion or indecision on the rebels' part, for no policy was served by letting them go and, once battle had become inevitable, Kett needed every one of his hostages. For Codd and Aldrich, however, this departure from the city was most timely: they were both in danger of being implicated in Kett's rebellious administration had they not been able to demonstrate, before the city was taken, their real commitment to the side of lawful authority. Now they received benefit of the general pardon and no charges of complicity in the rebellion were subsequently raised against them.

The fighting began when Warwick opened fire on St. Stephen's Gate and broke down the portcullis which obstructed it. A party of men led by Northampton and Captain Thomas Drury, a professional soldier,[1] forced an entry and began fighting the rebels in the neighbouring streets. At the same time Steward sent word to Warwick from within the city that the gate known as the Brazen Doors could easily be stormed and that he himself had caused St. Benedict's Gate to be opened. That Steward was able to do this shows again that for some reason Kett was not keeping close watch upon the leading citizens. A group of pioneers broke down the Brazen Doors while Warwick, with the body of the army, entered by St. Benedict's Gate some way to the north.

Warwick had now won the city, although the rebels remained within the walls in considerable numbers and street fighting continued throughout the afternoon. The Earl went at once to the market place and summarily hanged there forty-nine of the rebels who were unfortunate enough to be caught in the act of resisting the King's Lieutenant. Seeing this turn of events the loyal citizens who had stayed in Norwich came out of hiding to declare their obedience and secure for themselves the royal pardon. "To whom the Lord Lieutenant answered they should have pardon, and commanded every man home to his house, and to keep the same, and to take care that no rebels were therein sustained" (Sotherton).

Then Warwick suffered a foolish but serious accident. The bulk of his artillery and supplies had been left to enter the city after the army had secured a firm foothold and accordingly came in through St. Benedict's Gate at about three o'clock. Instead of turning right as they came down Benedict street, in order to reach the market place, they continued more or less straight on through Tombland, around the Cathedral, and along Bishopsgate street. Kett was still in control of the eastern ways out of Norwich and at once seized his chance. The errant guns and supplies were captured and on their way to the heath before Warwick knew they had arrived. Captain Drury was sent in pursuit and managed to do some damage to the retreating rebels, but the guns remained in Kett's possession.

Emboldened by this success the rebels in the city rallied for a counter attack. Dividing themselves into three companies they assembled at strategic points in the complex of streets in the centre of Norwich between Tombland and the market place, hoping to cut off parties of Warwick's soldiers from the main body. One such company was near St. Michael-at-Plea in Queen Street, a second by St. Simon and St. Jude's on Elm Hill, and a third at St. Andrew's Hall. Using these buildings (all of which still stand) as bases the rebels began to cause serious trouble. Several soldiers who strayed from the market place were ambushed and three or four of the gentlemen were killed. Hearing of this Warwick himself led a force to dispel the rebels, proceeding from the market place, past St. John Maddermarket, and turning right into St. Andrew's street. As they approached St. Andrew's Hall they were halted by vollies of arrows, but the arrival of Captain Drury, returning along Bishopsgate street from his vain pursuit of the artillery, took the rebels in the rear. Drury had with him a company of arquebusiers who returned the rebels' fire. The fighting was fierce and losses on both sides are estimated at as many as three hundred. According to Sotherton it lasted only half an hour, after which most of the rebels withdrew from the city to the heath.

Before they left, however, Kett's men managed to take more of Warwick's guns. These had been left in charge of a band of Welsh soldiers and were probably, on Warwick's orders, being moved up towards Bishop's Gate, for the defence of which they were intended, when the guards were surprised and outnumbered. The rebels were led, in this action, by one Miles, who succeeded in shooting the King's master gunner. The Welshmen withdrew and the guns and supplies fell to the rebels. Kett now had a considerable artillery. His guns were placed mostly outside Bishop's Gate and Conisford Gate. His advantage might not have been as great as it seems, however, because he probably had more guns than capable gunners.

At the end of the first day's fighting Warwick had made a number of mistakes and, for all his military experience, had fallen into the same trap as had formerly ensnared Northampton. He had brought his army into the city, with its maze of streets and miles of walls, and thus lost the advantage which maneuverability gives the trained soldier over the poorly-armed band of amateurs. Already the rebels had exploited the situation in a number of neat ambushes which had deprived Warwick of valuable guns and supplies and had apparently killed a number of his men. The rebels, working in smallish groups among the lanes, were striking swiftly and effectively as soon as Warwick made any move out of the market place where, by sheer force of numbers, he was safe. Only after heavy fighting and serious losses were these bands cleared from the streets. By nightfall on August 24 Warwick was in possession of Norwich, much as Northampton had been on the evening of July 31, with the rebel army intact biding its time on Mousehold. The only difference was that Warwick's force was several times greater than Northampton's had been, so that although it had been a serious error for the Marquess to try to defend the city it might not yet prove impossible for the Earl to do so.

The rebel tactics, at first sight, seem different on this occasion from those adopted in July on Northampton's approach, for then they had allowed the government forces to enter Norwich unopposed whereas against Warwick they closed the gates and put up some resistance. The resistance, however, was necessarily little more than a disorganized token. There was evidently no plan to hold the city, but rather to do what could be done to hinder and despoil the Earl's army before retreating to Mousehold. Kett's force at this time probably numbered between ten and fifteen thousand, only a fraction of which can possibly have been involved in the afternoon battle in the narrow streets between Tombland and the market place. The overall plan of the rebels was much as before: to wait until the royal army had settled itself in Norwich before making a concerted attack on the weak eastern defences. It was hoped that a series of such attacks would expend Warwick's strength and soon force him to a demoralised withdrawal. Kett could not afford to wait long, however, for the presence of a large hostile force in the city effectively cut off his main sources of supply: if Warwick should hold out for many days the rebel army would itself be forced to withdraw.

On the next day, Sunday August 25, Kett made a determined effort to break down Warwick's defences. The first attacks were made against the Conisford and Bishop's Gates, where Kett had concentrated his guns. Warwick realized that the Bishop's Gate was the weakest point of the city's perimeter and dispatched Lord Willoughby to command its defence. Warwick himself set up headquarters at Steward's house, holding the bulk of his forces in reserve nearby on the market place. About ten o'clock that morning word came to him that the rebels had broken through the Conisford Gate, fired the houses on Conisford street (now King street), and were at large in the southern section of the city. Merchandise stored at the common staithe had also been set afire. Forces were sent and the irruption of the rebels was checked. The fires were left burning because Warwick was unwilling to further deplete his reserves of troops in the city centre.

At more or less the same time an unexpected attack was made on the northern walls and a breach effected by the rebels somewhere between the Magdalen and Pockthorpe Gates. The rebels at one point occupied most of the section of the city north of the Wensum. Warwick's men succeeded in driving them out again, but not without losses: George Hastings, three of Captain Drury's gunners, and another unnamed gentleman were slain in this encounter and later buried, with other victims of the siege, in the churchyard of St. Martin-at-Place. As a precaution against further attacks from the north Warwick ordered the destruction of the bridges which joined the northern section to the rest of the city. In the sixteenth century there were four such bridges along the stretch of river enclosed by the northern wall: Whitefriars, Fye, Blackfriars, and Coslany. There are now seven bridges across this portion of the river, four of them on the sites of the old ones. The only bridge in Norwich of which the present structure is largely the same as it was in the time of the rising is the Bishopsgate bridge, which was then the only bridge crossing the river to the east of the city. The Whitefriars bridge seems actually to have been destroyed in accordance with these instructions, but protest from the citizens saved the others.

By this time it appeared to the citizens that Kett had the upper hand and that, even if Warwick were able to stand his ground, the damage resulting from continued fighting would be disastrous. To them, understandably, a government victory at the expense of their homes and property would not necessarily be preferable to a third surrender to the rebels. Some of them therefore advised Warwick to withdraw – not to abandon the campaign but to take his army out of the city and thereafter find some other battle-ground on which to meet the insurgents. This counsel, leaving aside its selfish motives, was not without strategic sense, for the city had already proved a trap to one royal army and it seemed that Warwick might well be expending more than he could afford in its defense. Kett would attack him only while he stayed in Norwich: on open ground Warwick's force would have every advantage over the rebels. On the other hand Warwick had no way of attacking Kett except through the city. If Warwick came out Kett would surely keep his force on the heights of Mouse-hold, maintaining a strategic advantage which would effectively cancel the superior training and weaponry of Warwick's soldiers. But if Warwick could hold Norwich for a few days Kett would probably have to come down for want of supplies. Warwick therefore decided to stay where he was, if possible, as the quickest way of achieving a solution. He must also have known that the fourteen hundred lanzknechts (German mercenaries), who in fact arrived next day, were close at hand.

In reply to the citizens Warwick "valiantly answered by God's grace not to depart the city, but would deliver it or leave his life" (Sotherton). He demanded a similar commitment from the citizens, and made them swear on their swords and by the cross that they would drive Kett out or die in the attempt. Once the city had been made as much a party to the conflict as the army Warwick proceeded to quarter his men, who so far had no regular accommodation in Norwich, upon the citizens. Once the house-holders realized that Warwick would not withdraw, that the siege would end either in victory or in complete destruction, they did whatever they could to provide for the soldiers. "Then did every man take forth his stuff and other things before hidden in places (to defend them from fire), to minister to the needs of these men" (Sotherton).

For the rest of the day the rebels were kept at bay. Warwick's arms, the bear and ragged staff, were set up on Steward's house. Both sides were entrenched and a temporary stalemate had been achieved.

On August 26 the mercenaries arrived while Warwick was at dinner, discharging their pieces to announce their presence. There were between one thousand and fourteen hundred of them, and many were accompanied by their wives. Seeing that Warwick's position was now even stronger than it had been when he successfully beat off their attack the day before the rebels decided to abandon Mousehold and risk a battle on open ground. The decision has been condemned as foolish, but it was inevitable. Once Norwich was effectively closed against them, as it had not been hitherto for any significant length of time, the rebels were themselves under siege in that their main supply lines were cut and in that they had nothing to fall back on but twenty miles of marshy country and the sea. Kett, or whoever now made the decisions in the camp, rightly concluded that Warwick could not be driven out of Norwich and that he would not come out voluntarily while the rebel army remained on the heath. The only course for Kett's men was to present themselves for a pitched battle on level ground. This would tempt Warwick out to meet them on more or less equal terms and so give them a chance of victory before starvation began to deplete their ranks.

Tradition has it that the rebels were encouraged to come down into the open by two rhymes which appeared to prophesy their victory if they did so.

> The country gnoffes
> Hob, Dick, and Hick,
> With clubs and clouted shoon
> Shall fill the vale
> Of Dussindale
> With slaughtered bodies soon.
>
> The heedless men within the dale
> Shall there be slain both great and small.[2]

There were reasons compelling enough for the move, however, without these grim foretellings. The whereabouts of Dussindale, named in the first rhyme and mentioned in the second, is no longer known: we cannot be sure exactly where the final conflict of Kett's rebellion took place. The indictment against Kett states that it was in the parishes of Sprowston and Thorpe. The most likely site is the low-lying ground outside the city walls to the northeast. Although the name no longer appears on the map the final battle is usually called Dussindale.

Not all the omens prior to battle favoured the rebels. As they were preparing to leave the heath a snake leapt from a rotten tree into the bosom of Mrs. Kett, an occurrence interpreted as distinctly unfavourable. (This is the only reference in the story to Kett's wife.) The departure proceeded nonetheless, and as a token of their resolution the rebels set fire to the many rough wooden shelters they had erected on the heath since their arrival six weeks before.

The march from Mousehold began on the night of Monday, August 26. The rebels wanted the cover of darkness not to hide their intentions from Warwick – the fires would make their movements clear – but to gain time to complete their maneuvres. Warwick might know what they were doing but he could scarcely attack before dawn: during the hours of darkness Kett hoped to bring his men to battle order and to make some kind of entrenchments. For it had evidently been decided that the rebels would fight defensively behind whatever obstacles could be found or constructed before Warwick's arrival on the field.

By morning the rebels had removed "their ordnance and munitions and all other things clean from that place they were in before, and devised trenches and stakes wherein they and theirs were entrenched, and set up great bulwarks of defense before and about, and placed their ordnance all about them. That the gentlemen, the prisoners, should not escape, they took them out of their prisons in Surrey Place, and carried them to the said Dussin's Dale with them, which was not past a mile off" (Sotherton). The prisoners were not to be a mere encumbrance on the battlefield: chained together they were placed before the front rank to provide a cover for Kett's men and to confuse the enemy.

When Warwick heard that the rebels had abandoned Mousehold he knew his chance had come and that he must strike as soon as possible, before Kett could prepare elaborate defences in Dussindale. Early next day, accompanied by the lords Northampton, Willoughby, Grey, and Bray, and by many of the gentry, he set off with the German mercenaries and all his cavalry, leaving the English foot soldiers to keep order in the city and to act as reserve troops. The army crossed Coslany bridge, left the city by St. Martin's Gate, turned to the right and continued around the north of the city until they came in sight of the rebels. Sir Edmund Knyvett, Sir Thomas Palmer, and two others were then sent forward with an offer of pardon to all, excepting the leaders, who would surrender at once. The offer was rejected and the battle began.

Miles, Kett's master gunner who had led the rebels in the capture of Warwick's artillery, shot and killed the royal standard bearer. Warwick ordered a charge of cavalry on Kett's ranks despite the screen of prisoners behind which the rebels were sheltered. The charge broke the rebel lines and the mercenaries fired supporting volleys into the defenders. Kett's front rank was put to flight. The prisoners, all of whom are said miraculously to have survived the onslaught, were now able to make their escape. The battle soon became a rout. A party of rebels rallied and made a stand behind barricades improvised from carts and wagons. Warwick mercifully sent a Herald to repeat the offer of pardon. There was no reason, other than humanity, for the Earl to offer pardon again at this stage in the proceedings, and the rebels were understandably suspicious, unable to believe the offer could be genuine. They replied that they would indeed surrender if Warwick would in person guarantee the offer of pardon. Warwick duly appeared, confirmed the promise, and had the Herald read the King's commission and grant of pardon to all who surrendered. This, at four o'clock on the afternoon of Tuesday, August 27, was the end of Kett's rebellion.

Slain in the battle were Robert Knyvett (son of Charles Knyvett and kinsman to Sir Edmund), Thomas Wodehouse (a priest), and six other gentlemen, all buried in St. Peter Mancroft in Norwich. Overall Warwick may have lost some two hundred and fifty men on this occasion. Kett's losses in the battle were much heavier and are not known precisely. Estimates range from two thousand (Edward VI) to three thousand five hundred (Holinshed). Three thousand altogether may have perished at Dussindale which, although briefly told, was no mere skirmish.

In Norwich there was great rejoicing. The soldiers had won their victory and the citizens were restored to the lawful enjoyment of their properties and privileges after six weeks of disorder, deprivation, and uncertainty. All booty taken from the rebels was distributed among the soldiers who sold it on the city market place. The Corporation provided two barrels of beer which were drunk at the market cross by the soldiers returning from the field.

19. *After the battle*

Robert Kett left the battlefield early in the afternoon when the defeat of his forces was obviously inevitable. He rode off alone in a roughly northwesterly direction and by evening had travelled some ten miles to the village of Swannington. Why he took this direction is not clear. If he had any purpose at all it may have been to reach one of the small ports on the north Norfolk coast and to make his escape by sea. (Had he continued in the direction he was going he would have come to Wells, which was a sizeable port in those days.) He seems to have stopped at Swannington only because he was tired, probably having missed sleep on the previous night in order to direct the move from Mousehold to Dussindale. At any rate he made no attempt to do anything there but simply stopped to rest in a barn. He was seen and recognized by men unloading hay from a cart, who seized him and took him to the house of Master Richards. There he stayed the night, was fed, well treated, and made no attempt to elude his light captivity. Word of his whereabouts had been sent to Warwick in Norwich and twenty horsemen were sent next morning to bring Kett back. On February 3, 1550, by order of the Privy Council, twenty shillings was paid to the man who first apprehended Kett.

That morning, August 28, the executions began in Norwich. Nine of the more notable rebels, including Miles the gunner, were partly hanged, disembowelled alive, beheaded and quartered, according to the custom of the time, which prescribed this grim end to those convicted of high treason. The ritual was performed, with deliberate irony, at the Oak of Reformation. The heads of the nine rebels were taken and "fixed on the tops of the towers of the city, the rest of the body bestowed upon several places, and set up to the terror of others" (Sotherton). The exhibition of the corpses was not gratuitous barbarism but an essential part of judicial execution, the purpose of which was not so much to torment the condemned man as to make his case an effective example to others. More rebels were hanged on the gallows outside the Magdalen Gate, but when and how many cannot be known for certain. Warwick had already executed forty-nine on the day of his first entry into Norwich – obviously in order to quell resistance in the city. Estimates of those executed after the battle begin at thirty and rise as high as three hundred. Recent writers have condemned the punishment as excessive, but to do so is unhistorical. All those found to have supported Kett were guilty of treason and therefore stood by law to lose their lives unless covered by the royal pardon. Only those few who had surrendered either before the battle of Dussindale or in response to Warwick's personal offer at the end of the day were so covered: the others, the great majority who had either fled the field or been captured in the fighting, were unquestionably guilty of crimes legally punishable by death. Warwick was bound to make some kind of judicial reprisal after the rebels had been dispersed. He could not ignore and allow to go unpunished the loss of life, destruction of property, desecration of churches, and defiance of the King's representatives for which Kett's men had been responsible.

The rebels had indeed assembled for purposes fundamentally honest, even honourable, and had themselves, in the beginning at least, tried to reform their opponents rather than to eliminate them. But such arguments carried little weight in Tudor England where there were no crimes greater than disruption of civil order. Warwick's dealings with the rebels, seen in the context of the times, were surprisingly lenient. Only thirteen years before, after the Pilgrimage of Grace, in spite of pardons granted, Henry VIII had ordered against the inhabitants of the north reprisals which amounted to massacre in some areas: two hundred and sixteen judicial executions are recorded and many more of the common people perished in the villages of Cumberland. Tradition credits Warwick with deliberately keeping executions after Kett's rebellion to the minimum consistent with contemporary notions of justice. "Many of the gentlemen, carried away with displeasure and desire of revenge, laboured to stir up the mind of Warwick to cruelty. Not contented with the punishment of a few they would have rooted out utterly the offspring and wicked race of them, and were so eager and earnest in it that they constrained Warwick to use speech unto them openly" (Sotherton). Warwick restrained the gentry with two arguments in particular: that mercy should have some place in the administration of the law, and that if all the rebels were executed the local economy would be seriously upset by the consequent shortage of labour.

That night the dead were buried, for fear of the plague, outside the Magdalen Gate.

Next day, August 29, Warwick, his officers, and a great crowd of gentry and citizens met for a service of thanksgiving in the church of St. Peter Mancroft. The service was held in St. Peter's (which overlooks the market place) rather than the Cathedral no doubt because it was intended primarily to offer the thanks of the city: St. Peter's is the greatest and most central of the many city churches, whereas the Cathedral is the seat of the Bishop and the church of the diocese. Later, on the advice of Thomas Thirlby, who became Bishop of Norwich in the following year, this service of thanksgiving became an annual event held on August 27, the day of Dussindale. The tradition persisted for over a hundred years, for there is record of such a service being held as late as 1667.

Warwick remained in Norwich until September 7, primarily occupied in the meantime with settlement of disputes over property which had arisen in the wake of the rebellion. The problems were many: distributing property, deciding claims for compensation, hearing accusations, and disposing of prisoners convicted. The extent and complexity of this business is suggested by a letter written at this time by Vice Admiral Sir Thomas Wodehouse to his brother, Sir William, in London.

> Brother:
>
> You shall understand that my lord of Warwick does execution of many men at Norwich. And the gentlemen crave at his hand the gift of the riches of them, and do daily bring in men by accusation. But I have neither accused any man, nor yet have asked the gift of any, although I am spoiled of 2000 sheep and all my bullocks and horses with the most part of my corn in the country. All the ordinance and spoil that was taken in the Camp is the King's. I moved my lord for my 2 pieces of brass but I cannot have them at his hands yet he is very gentle to me. Raffe Symondes made a great complaint of Turcoke to my lord, and yet he was in the Camp but 2 days in the beginning, and then went to Newcastle and came not home again till the battle was done. Notwithstanding the sheriff seized all his goods, and if I had not made earnest suit to my lord, he had lost his goods and been in danger of death. I pray you write to me if you think it meet that I come up. There is a Commission come down of Oyer determinate; we have many prisoners at Yarmouth. There is in the Commission my Lord Willoughby, my Lord Wentworth, Sir Edmund Wyndham, Sir John Clere, with other gentlemen, and yet I am left out. Yet there be in my charge at Yarmouth seven or eight score prisoners, and they shall sit upon the delivery of them.... Thus fare ye well from Waxham the 3 of September."[1]

In little more than a week Warwick could scarcely have heard all the cases himself, but he must have provided principles and guidelines whereby the local courts could deal with these matters after his departure. The city was most grateful to the Earl for his services: his arms were set up beside the royal arms at all of the gates.

Where Warwick stayed during the days after the battle is not certain. Steward's house provided a good headquarters so long as military affairs were in progress, but once the fighting was over Warwick may well have moved to more spacious accommodation. It is possible that he resided again at Sir Thomas Gresham's house at Intwood. Some time was found for leisure and social intercourse with the local gentry, for during his days in or near Norwich the Earl's son Robert met and fell in love with Amy Robsart, daughter and heiress of a Norfolk gentleman. Amy, who was only seventeen in 1549, would hardly have encountered Robert Dudley except at the house of one of her relatives. Since Warwick and his sons are known to have passed at least one night at Intwood it has been suggested that this or nearby Stanfield Hall was the scene of their first acquaintance.

Amy's father, Sir John Robsart of Syderstone, who had been Sheriff of Norfolk and Suffolk in 1547, had married Elizabeth, the widow of Roger Appleyard of Stanfield. Elizabeth was the mother of four children by her first husband, including the brothers John and Philip Appleyard who were captured by Kett and who later helped to defend Norwich against the rebels. Amy Robsart, born in 1532, was therefore half-sister to the Appleyards of Stanfield.[2] Elizabeth, who by the terms of her late husband's will held Stanfield Hall for life, died at some time during the year of the rising, and Stanfield, only three miles from Wymondham, passed to her eldest son John. Amy might well have been living at Stanfield prior to her mother's death and could well have visited her half-brother's family there afterwards. She was evidently in the neighbourhood of Norwich in August and September of 1549.

Stanfield figures in the story of Kett's rebellion not only in connection with Robert Dudley's first unfortunate marriage but also as the residence from which John Flowerdew had conducted his demolition of Wymondham Abbey. Elizabeth Robsart's house was two or three miles closer to Wymondham than Flowerdew's home at Hethersett and was open to the Sergeant because his eldest son William was married to Frances Appleyard, Elizabeth's daughter. The Appleyards and the Flowerdews were neighbours, relations, and allies, and were all involved from the earliest days as the objects of Kett's hostility.

Robert Dudley and Amy Robsart were married at Somerset's palace at Sheen on June 4, 1550, the day after Robert's elder brother John, Warwick's eldest son, had there married Somerset's daughter Anne. Sir John Robsart gave them his manor of Syderstone in northwest Norfolk, where it is supposed they spent the first years of their marriage. Warwick settled on them Coxford Priory and other lands in the county which he had been granted out of the estates of the attainted Duke of Norfolk. In 1553 he also

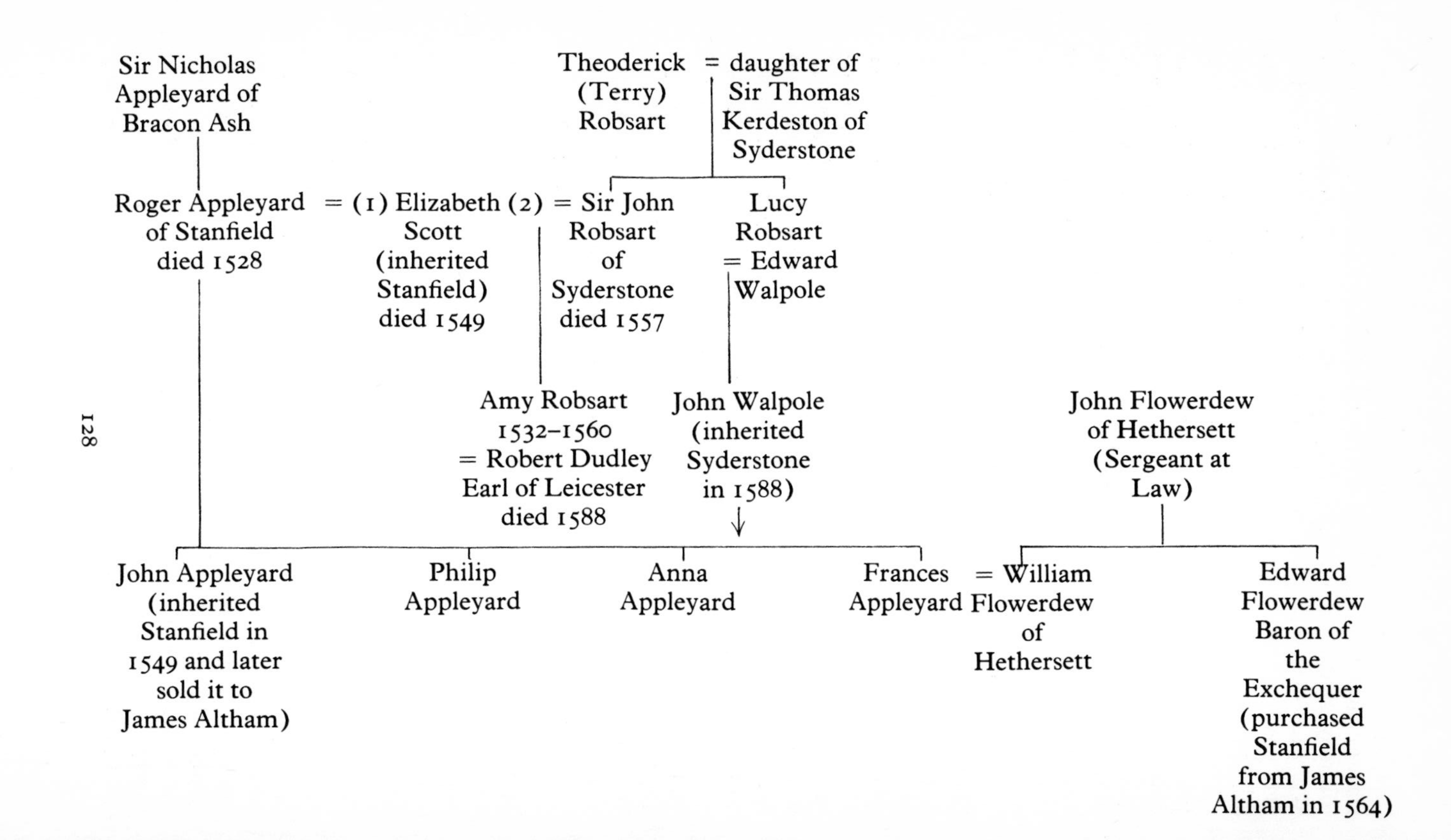

Sir Nicholas Appleyard of Bracon Ash
Theoderick (Terry) Robsart
= daughter of Sir Thomas Kerdeston of Syderstone
Roger Appleyard of Stanfield died 1528
= (1) Elizabeth (2) Scott (inherited Stanfield) died 1549
= Sir John Robsart of Syderstone died 1557
Lucy Robsart = Edward Walpole
Amy Robsart 1532–1560 = Robert Dudley Earl of Leicester died 1588
John Walpole (inherited Syderstone in 1588)
John Flowerdew of Hethersett (Sergeant at Law)
John Appleyard (inherited Stanfield in 1549 and later sold it to James Altham)
Philip Appleyard
Anna Appleyard
Frances Appleyard
= William Flowerdew of Hethersett
Edward Flowerdew Baron of the Exchequer (purchased Stanfield from James Altham in 1564)

gave them the manor of Hemsby, near Yarmouth.

The rest of the story has often been told. Ten years later Dudley had become the favourite of the young Queen Elizabeth who, it was generally thought, wished to marry him. His wife Amy was an obstacle to any such plan, and when on September 8, 1560, she was found with a broken neck at the foot of a staircase at Cumnor Place in Berkshire (where she had been residing) it was immediately suspected that either her husband or the Queen or both had contrived her death. As soon as Dudley heard the news he saw that suspicion would fall on him and did everything he could to promote a disinterested inquiry. John Appleyard was summoned to Cumnor, as the representative of Amy's family, and was present at her funeral while Dudley remained carefully in London. Eventually the Berkshire coroner's court returned a verdict of death by misadventure and Dudley was, officially at least, removed from suspicion.

John Appleyard was not satisfied and in 1567 he made an effort to reopen the issue. Seven years had passed, however, and Dudley, who had long since been restored to favour and created Earl of Leicester, had then nothing to fear from Amy's ghost. Appleyard was ordered to drop the matter and to apologize for his accusations. Amy's marriage into the powerful Dudley family, although no doubt hailed as a great match, brought her Norfolk relations into trouble on several occasions. In 1553 John Appleyard had supported his brother-in-law when that nobleman proclaimed Jane Grey Queen on King's Lynn market place. Later Amy's death alienated her Norfolk relations from Dudley and placed them in the difficult position of having to take some action against one who had become the most powerful man in the kingdom. The Appleyards seem to have survived and prospered in Norfolk, however, for in 1588 (coincidentally the year of Leicester's death) John was appointed High Sheriff of the county.

The marriage of Robert Dudley and Amy Robsart was almost certainly, unlike the political matches of his brothers and sisters, a love-affair which had its origins in the relaxation of the days in Norwich after Kett's defeat. But while Robert Dudley went courting Robert Kett and his brother William were kept under close guard in Norwich. When Warwick left for London the Ketts were placed in the keeping of Thomas Audley, who was paid fifty pounds from the treasury in reward for his successful delivery of the captives to the Tower of London. The Ketts were in the Tower by September 9, and there they were to remain until the end of November. William, whose lesser role in the rebellion was generally acknowledged, was allowed freedom within the confines of the fortress, but Robert was kept in a cell. On October 14 they were joined in the Tower by Edward Seymour, Duke of Somerset, arrested by order of the Council which was now dominated by the Earl of Warwick.

20. *The Fall of Somerset*

The fall of the Protectorate in October, 1549, belongs to the story of the Norfolk rebellion because the uprisings of that summer had not only demonstrated the failure of Somerset's domestic policies but also given his opponents the means to effect his overthrow. The Norfolk rebellion was the most serious of these risings and, unlike that in the west, it was concerned almost exclusively with agrarian and legal matters, the very matters upon which Somerset was meeting strong opposition within the Council. It was Warwick, moreover, the victor of Dussindale, and not Russell or Herbert, who led the Council in the confrontation with the Protector.

By the autumn of 1549 there was strong feeling against Somerset among the lords and gentry and especially among his fellow councillors. The failure of the enclosure policy, against which many councillors had protested and as a result of which some of their properties had suffered riotous attacks, was the deepest grievance but was not the only cause of dissent. Somerset had of late become increasingly aloof, increasingly inclined to act without consulting the Council, and increasingly brusque in his official relations with his colleagues. Although the Protectorate had been designed, with the Council's approval, to place considerable powers in the hands of one man, it was felt that Somerset had exceeded the spirit of the institution and was unduly inclined to personal rule. It was never seriously suggested, even by his enemies, that the Duke had any treasonable intention to retain his power beyond the King's minority. The evidence, on the contrary, indicates that Somerset took his responsibilities to the constitution with all due seriousness and that his natural austerity made him impatient of consulting others in the execution of what he saw as his duty. Had his policies been even moderately successful he might well have held his office until it was ended naturally either by Edward's death or his coming of age, but the disasters at home after a series of failures abroad caused the Council to insist on a greater part in the direction of affairs.

Besides Somerset's official conduct several lesser irritants are usually mentioned as factors in his downfall. His second wife, Anne Stanhope, although loyally devoted to him, is said to have hurt her husband's standing by her proud demeanour and tendency to interfere in political matters. Somerset was also accused of accumulating great wealth through his office, although the figures do not suggest that the Protector's income was, by the standards of the time, disproportionate to his rank. The basis for the criticism was probably his extensive building projects, especially that of Somerset House, which fell necessarily under the public gaze. The Duke was also engaged on the complete reconstruction on a new site of the Seymour family home of Wolf Hall in Wiltshire and on the building of Syon House (which still stands, the only one of these projects completed in his lifetime). The construction of Somerset House is said to have aroused particular ill-feeling because it involved the destruction of a number of old dwellings, some belonging to noblemen and senior churchmen, and of some church buildings, including part of the cloister of St. Paul's.

A more serious cause of Somerset's loss of credit was the affair of his brother Thomas, Lord Seymour of Sudeley, executed for treason in March of that year. Seymour, a reckless and unstable character, was highly jealous of his elder brother's power and dignity, in which he thought his own share, as another uncle of the King, should be much greater. He tried several ways of increasing his own wealth and importance, including an attempt to seduce the Princess Elizabeth, a plot to marry the King to Jane Grey and gain hold over the young couple, and the use of his office of Lord High Admiral to foster piracy and share in its proceeds. He was finally arrested in January of 1549 and eventually found guilty of originating an absurd but dangerous plot to win control of the King's person. Somerset could certainly have saved his brother's life, but the Protector's austerity prevented him from securing for his family favours he would not have granted to others. Yet the very fact that the Protector could have deflected the course of Tudor justice made his failure to do so in the case of a brother seem to most men unnatural.

Most serious, however, was the fact that the Protector's agrarian policies, opposed all along by his colleagues, had resulted in widespread disturbance, and that the disturbance had been put down, not by Somerset himself, but by those who had cause to oppose him. If Somerset had led an army against the rebels he would probably have saved his position, for in so doing he would in effect have publicly disavowed and rectified his controversial policies and, at the same time, have held control of a substantial military force. As it was he did nothing but issue ill-informed and sometimes offensive orders to the men in the field: he was not directly involved in the military activities of July and August and by September there were left under his direct command only some five hundred household troops. The military strength of the realm was directly controlled by men who were then his political enemies.

Sir William Herbert, like many of the gentry, had suffered damage and loss from the enclosure riots, and now Herbert was joint commander of the largest force in the country. Russell, the other commander, had evidently been much offended by Somerset's criticisms of his handling of the western situation. Warwick may also have been the recipient of letters from the Protector critical of his military conduct (although none have survived), and he may have been offended by Somerset's failure to grant his son Ambrose certain offices on their return to London after the victory. The chief reasons for Warwick's opposition, however, would seem not to have been personal but rather based on a perception that the Protectorate had failed and that the time was ripe for a man such as himself to bring about its dissolution.

The general feeling was represented to Somerset by Paget, his colleague and advisor, by whose assistance, at the time of the old King's death, the Protectorate had been created. Paget remained loyal to the Duke to the end, but seeing clearly the Protector's failings he was never afraid to warn him openly against them. One of the last of several admonitory letters from Paget was written on July 7, 1549, as rebellions were breaking out all over England. The letter intentionally expresses the feeling among the lords and landowners with respect to the domestic policies of the Protectorate.

> I told your Grace the truth, and was not believed: well, now your Grace sees it what says your Grace? Marry, the King's subjects out of all discipline, out of obedience, caring neither for Protector nor King, and much less for any other mean officer. And what is the cause? Your own levity, your softness, your opinion to be good to the poor. I know, I say, your good meaning and honest nature. But I say, Sir, it is great pity (as the common proverb goes in a warm summer) that ever fair weather should do harm. It is pity that your so much gentleness should be an occasion of so great an evil as is now chanced in England by these rebels. ... I know in this matter of the commons every man of the Council has misliked your proceedings, and wished it otherwise.[1]

Somerset was held directly responsible for the civil chaos of that summer, and his failure to take firm and open control of military operations against the rebellious commons was taken as final evidence of his commitment to unpractical policies.

Exactly when Warwick decided to organize the growing distrust of Somerset's administration into an effective political force for his overthrow cannot be determined. He seems to have been sincerely cooperative with the Protector, in spite of occasional differences of opinion, until his departure for Norfolk. Shortly after his return to London in mid September, however, he was meeting with the Catholic lords Southampton and Arundel, obviously in order to win their support for a broadly based opposition to the Protector. There was nothing underhanded in the conspiracy which followed: Warwick's meetings with the Catholic lords and with other members of the Council were known to Somerset, and the coming breach in the administration was apparent to political observers. On September 15, for instance, the Imperial Ambassador Van der Delft reported the division in the Council and the growing political hostility between Somerset and Warwick.[2]

Somerset's first recorded reaction came ten days later: on September 25 he sent an order to Russell and Herbert, still commanding the great army in the west, to return at once to London. Control of this army was vital. Somerset's order is plainly an effort to bring its commanders under his authority before they could be persuaded to join Warwick. Warwick's army had partially disbanded after Kett's defeat, but its professional core had returned to the London area and still acknowledged the Earl's authority. The force, small though it was, greatly outnumbered the few hundred guards which the Protector could command. If Warwick and his associates were prepared to use force Somerset's best chance of withstanding them lay with the army of the west.

Somerset was probably too late with his order of September 25. The leaders of the western army, Lord Russell and Sir William Herbert, were already disposed against him and, although no direct evidence survives, they had probably already received overtures from Warwick. Whilst awaiting some sign from the west Somerset made an attempt to disperse the forces of his opponents. As Protector he still had great powers which might yet win the game: he controlled the person of the King, he had the exercise of royal authority, and was (in principle) supreme commander of the English armies. On September 30 he issued a proclamation:

> The King's most excellent majesty, with the advice and assent of his dearest uncle the Lord Protector, his majesty's Lieutenant General of all his armies, and the rest of his highness' council, straightly chargeth and commandeth that all manner of soldiers, as well Englishmen as strangers, of what nation soever they be, having had and received his highness' wages, or prests, and thereupon assigned to repair to the parts of the north or elsewhere to serve his majesty, that forthwith, upon proclamation hereof, without further tarrying or delay, they and every of them not only avoid and depart forth of the city of London and

> the suburbs of the same but also that, according to the several wages and payments to them advanced, they with all diligence and competent journeys repair where they and every of them are appointed to serve the King's majesty; as they will answer the King's majesty at their most extreme perils to the contrary.[3]

Had this order been obeyed the forces loyal to Warwick would have been removed to the remote regions of the north where their effect on the political crisis would have been negligible. As it was, however, with this proclamation ignored and still no word from Russell and Herbert, the Protector was obliged to take defensive measures.

Somerset's greatest strength in this adversity lay in his deserved popularity with the commons, a popularity which had survived the conflicts of the summer months largely because the Duke had not openly acted against the commons or renounced his lenient anti-enclosure policies. He could therefore expect a considerable response to a general appeal for help against such unpopular figures as Warwick, Russell, and Herbert, the men who had put down the risings and supervised the consequent executions. Accordingly another proclamation was drawn up on October 1.

> The King's majesty straightly chargeth and commandeth all his loving subjects with all haste to repair to his highness at his majesty's manor of Hampton Court, in most defensible array, with harness and weapons, to defend his most royal person, and his most entirely beloved uncle the Lord Protector, against whom certain hath attempted a most dangerous conspiracy; and this to do in all possible haste.[4]

An appeal to the commons, already thoroughly unsettled, would undoubtedly have brought results, but Somerset was hesitant to make such an appeal for fear of precipitating a civil war. Publication of this proclamation was witheld for five days until October 5, on which day further orders were sent to Russell and Herbert, who had still made no response, commanding them to come at once to defend the King and the Protector at Hampton Court. At this time Somerset was planning to hold his ground at Hampton Court, and to this end he placed guards around it that night.

Next day several thousand commoners responded in person to the call for a general array. That so many came so soon suggests that had the Duke made a serious effort to recruit forces from the countryside he could have amassed a large army without difficulty. At first Somerset divided these men into companies and disposed them for the defense of Hampton Court, but towards evening he realized that the palace was indefensible. He decided to move at once, with the King, to Windsor Castle, which had the added advantage of being further from London and closer to the hoped-for aid from the west. A letter was sent to Russell that evening telling him of the change of place.

While making preparations for defensive action Somerset did not neglect to open diplomatic communications with Warwick and his associates, who by now included the great majority of the Council. On October 6 he sent Sir William Petre to negotiate, but Petre threw in his lot with Warwick and never returned. Even so, an exchange of letters began soon after, and while both sides conducted acrimonious and inaccurate propaganda campaigns over the next few days these private letters gradually worked towards a peaceful settlement. Somerset's only supporters of note were Archbishop Cranmer, Paget, and Sir Thomas Smith. On October 8 Russell and Herbert at last declared themselves, with some circumlocution, to be for Warwick, and on the next day the Protector announced his willingness to surrender.

The western army had advanced to within forty miles of Windsor. On October 9, however, it withdrew somewhat, for fear of provoking popular uprisings in Somerset's favour. Although both sides were now in virtual agreement Somerset's surrender had to be managed with great caution if civil disturbance was to be avoided. On October 10 commissioners from the Council read letters in the presence of the King at Windsor proclaiming Somerset a traitor, but at the same time private assurance was given that he would not be punished or persecuted. Next day Sir Anthony Wingfield went from London with five hundred horsemen to arrest the Duke at Windsor, and three days later, on October 14, Somerset was taken to the Tower where he was formally charged under thirty-one articles, of which he acknowledged twenty-nine.

A fine was imposed on Somerset, but apparently never collected. In less than four months he was free and fully pardoned. By April, 1550, he was back on the Council and there is no doubt that, had he avoided further intrigue, he might have suffered no further from his fall. As it was, he was found guilty of subsequently plotting against Warwick and the Council and was executed in 1552.

21. *Kett's Trial*

Kett and his brother were in the Tower from September 9 until November 29 when, having been convicted of treason, they were taken back to Norfolk for execution. The Duke of Somerset was taken to the Tower only five days after Kett and was still there when Kett died. The former rebel and the former Protector had each in a way contributed to the other's undoing, and had done so, ironically, each through an over-zealous pursuit of agrarian reforms. They had both, besides, been defeated by the same man, the Earl of Warwick, who had replaced Kett as virtual dictator in Norwich and who was about to replace Somerset as leader of the governing Council.

The story of Kett's final weeks is unsatisfying because we have no utterance at all from the man who stands at the centre of the Norfolk rising but whose character is almost wholly concealed. Apart from the plea of guilty entered at his trial history records no word or action of Kett's from the moment of his captivity. He must have made certain preparations for death, he may have seen his family and friends, he perhaps made some statement of his case — but none of this has come down to us. All we have are the official documents of the trial and the facts of the execution.

Kett was in prison for six weeks, during which time the country put itself in order after the rebellions and the fall of the Protector's government. At last, on November 23, a commission of Oyer and Terminer was issued under the great seal appointing six judges for the trial of Robert and William Kett.

EDWARD THE SIXTH, by the Grace of God, King of England, France, and Ireland, Defender of the Faith, and on earth of the church of England and Ireland Supreme Head, to our beloved and faithful Richard Lister, Knight; Edward Montagu, Knight; Richard Cholmeley, Knight; Edmund Mervyn, Knight; William Portman, Knight; and John Hinde, Knight; Greeting:

WHEREAS ... William Kett, otherwise called William Knight, late of Wymondham, in the county of Norfolk, mercer; and Robert Kett, otherwise called Robert Knight, late of Wymondham, in the county of Norfolk, tanner; in the presence of our beloved and faithful Edward North, Knight; John Baker, Knight; and Richard Southwell, Knight, three of our Council; concerning various high treasons, by the aforesaid ... William Kett and Robert Kett supposed to have been committed, having been examined by the said Edward North, John Baker, and Richard Southwell, and on the aforesaid examinations concerning the same treasons are, and each one of them is, vehemently suspected, as we have learnt from the relation and testimony of the aforesaid Edward North, John Baker, and Richard Southwell, delivered into our Court of Chancery: KNOW YE THEREFORE, that we, fully confiding in your fidelity, industry, and provident circumspection, according to the form of the Statute in this case made and provided, have assigned you, or four of you, our justices, to enquire by oath of honest and lawful men of our county of Middlesex, and by other ways, modes, and means by which you will better discover, or may be able to discover more fully the truth, as well within your liberties as without, by whom the truth of the affair may be better discovered, concerning all treasons, misprisions of treason, and murders, and each of them, by ... William Kett and Robert Kett, as well within our counties of ... Norfolk, Suffolk ... and Essex, as also within the said county of Middlesex, or within any one of them, in any way had, done, perpetrated, or committed: And concerning other articles and circumstances relating to the premises or to any one of them, or in any way to any or any one of them; and to hear and determine the same treasons and other premises according to the law and custom of our realm of England, and according to the form and effect of the aforesaid statute in this case made and provided: AND therefore we charge you that on certain days, within the aforesaid county of Middlesex, you, or four of you, in order to see this, meet at Westminister, in the aforesaid county of Middlesex, and hear and determine diligently the inquisitions made upon the premises, and all and every the premises; and do and complete them in the form aforesaid, doing therein what belongs to justice, according to the law and custom of our realm of England, and the aforesaid Statute in this case made and provided, our fines and other things to us belonging being secured to us: We further charge, by the tenor of these presents, our Sheriff of Middlesex, that on certain days which you, or four of you, shall have caused him to know of, he bring before you, or four of you, so many honest and lawful men of his bailiwick, as well within the liberties as without, by whom the truth of the matter in the premises may be the better known and inquired into.[1]

The Statute mentioned several times in the Commission is that of 25 Edw III (1352) defining treason and its proper punishment. This Statute had been replaced by much severer laws under Henry VII and his son, but had been restored by Somerset's "great repealer", the Statute of 1 Edw VI, c. 12, in which the Protector had attempted, in his first Parliament, to win support for his new government and express disapproval of the rigour of the previous administration by enacting certain legal relaxations and allowing a measure of religious toleration.

The jury duly returned by the Sheriff of Middlesex consisted of Richard Brine, John Barnes, William Lowe, John Coke Sadler, Miles Child, Clement Dawes, John Hunsdon de Lane, Thomas Ward, Roger à Wood, Edward Gregory, William Rayner, Richard Brown, Thomas Shepherd, William Pay of Sudbury, and John Sadgrove. Two days later the justices appointed for the trial sent to Sir John Gage, Constable of the Tower, to require the delivery of his prisoners Robert and William Kett at eight o'clock next morning to stand trial at Westminster. The prisoners were delivered and the trial was held on Tuesday, November 26, 1549. Both men pleaded guilty and offered no defence. Concerning William Kett the court found that he,

> not having God before his eyes, but seduced by diabolical instigation, and not weighing his due allegiance; And also as a felonious, and malicious traitor, and a public enemy against our most mighty and serence Lord, Edward VIth, by the grace of God King of England, France, and Ireland, Defender of the Faith, and on earth of the Church of England and Ireland Supreme Head, feloniously, maliciously, and traitoriously intending and plotting utterly to destroy and annihilate that hearty love and obedience which all true and faithful subjects of our said Lord the King that now is of this realm of England, bear, and are rightly held to bear, towards the same our Lord the King; And to excite sedition, rebellion, and insurrection between the same our Lord the King and his faithful subjects; And in order to perfect and accomplish his said felonious, malicious, and traitorous intention, and wicked purposes, to the peril of our said Lord the King that now is, and the subversion of this his realm of England, according to his power, against his due allegiance, did, on the 16th day of August, in the 3rd year of the reign of Edward VIth, by the grace of God King of England, France, and Ireland, Defender of the Faith, and on earth of the Church of England and Ireland Supreme Head, and on the two days then next ensuing, at Mounty Surrey, in the parish of Thorpe, near Norwich, in the said county of Norfolk, and at divers other

places within the county aforesaid, by traitorous proclamations, and hue and cry, there being adherent and gathered to him, unlawfully and traitorously, Robert Kett and very many malefactors there, to the number of 20,000 persons, as felonious traitors, enemies, and public rebels against our said most dread and excellent Lord the King that now is, Edward VIth, of their unanimous and traitorous assent and consent, with banners unfurled, swords, shields, clubs, cannon, halberts, lances, bows, arrows, breast-plates, coats of mail, caps, helmets, and other arms offensive and defensive, in warlike manner armed and arrayed, feloniously and traitorously make an insurrection and levy war against our same Lord the King that now is; and throughout the whole of that 16th day of August, and the said two days then next ensuing, in order to accomplish their traitorous design aforesaid, did himself, with the aforesaid Robert and other traitors and rebels, at Mount Surrey aforesaid, and elsewhere in the county of Norfolk, with force of arms aforesaid, traitorously assemble, confederate, and conspire together, by war and in warlike manner, to destroy the people of our said Lord the King that now is of this his realm of England: And further, the Jurors aforesaid present that the aforesaid William Kett, on the 20th day of August, in the said 3rd year of our said Lord the King that now is, on Mousehold Heath, in the parish of Thorpe aforesaid, in the said county of Norfolk, did feloniously and traitorously give to the same Robert Kett and the said other traitors, then and there being, comfort, aid, and counsel in their traitorous and wicked designs, and in levying war against our same Lord the King, against his due allegiance, and against the peace of our said Lord the King that now is, his crown and dignity, and against the form of the Statute in this case lately made and provided.[2]

Concerning Robert Kett it was found that he,

not having God before his eyes, but seduced by diabolical instigation, and not weighing his due allegiance; And also as a felonious and malicious traitor, and a public enemy, against our most mighty and serene Lord, Edward VIth, by the grace of God King of England, France, and Ireland, Defender of the Faith, and on earth of the Church of England and Ireland Supreme Head, feloniously, maliciously, and traitorously intending and plotting utterly to destroy and annihilate that hearty love and obedience which all true and faithful subjects of our said Lord the King that now is of this his realm of England, bear and are rightly held to bear towards the same our Lord the King: and to excite sedition, rebellion, and insurrection between the same our Lord the King and his faithful subjects;

and to deprive the same our Lord the King of his dignity, honours, and pre-eminences; and in order to perfect and accomplish his said felonious and traitorous intention and wicked purposes, to the peril of our said Lord the King that now is, and the subversion of this his realm of England, according to his power, contrary to his due allegiance, on the 20th day of July, in the 3rd year of the reign of Edward VI, by the grace of God, King of England, France, and Ireland, Defender of the Faith, and on earth of the Church of England and Ireland Supreme Head; and continuously, after the said 20th day of July for six weeks then next ensuing, on Mousehold Heath, in the parish of Thorpe, near Norwich, in the county of Norfolk, and at divers other places in the said county of Norfolk, by traitorous proclamations, hue and cry, and the ringing of bells, very many malefactors being adherent and collecting to him to the number of twenty thousand; did, as felons, traitors, enemies, and public rebels against our said most dread and excellent Lord the King that now is, Edward VI, of their unanimous assent and consent, with banners unfurled, swords, shields, clubs, cannon, halberts, lances, bows, arrows, breast-plates, coats of mail, caps, helmets, and other arms offensive and defensive, armed and arrayed in warlike manner, traitorously make an insurrection and levy war against the same our Lord the King that now is: And he traitorously caused some writings and bills then and there to be written and subscribed, as well to excite and procure the lieges of our said Lord the King in the said county of Norfolk, to levy open war against the same our Lord the King; as also to rob and spoil the true and faithful subjects of the said our Lord the King. And the aforesaid Robert Kett, with the aforesaid traitors and rebels, during all that 20th day of July, and the six weeks then next ensuing, to carry out their traitorous intention aforesaid, together on Mousehold Heath aforesaid, in the county of Norfolk aforesaid, and in divers other places in the same county of Norfolk, with the aforesaid force of arms, assembled themselves, confederated and conspired together, by war and in warlike manner to destroy the people of our said Lord the King that now is of this his realm of England: And very many faithful subjects of our said Lord the King that now is, viz. knights, esquires, and gentlemen of the said county of Norfolk, at Mount Surrey, in the said county of Norfolk, did they feloniously and traitorously imprison; and in that prison for a long time feloniously and traitorously detain them, crying and shouting out with these words:

Kill the Gentlemen.

And very many faithful subjects of our said Lord the King that

> now is, in the same county of Norfolk, did they traitorously despoil of their goods and chattels, the same 20th day of July and during the said six weeks then next ensuing; and by force of arms did they traitorously take and carry them off; and very many faithful subjects of our said Lord the King that now is, who were under the rule and conduct of the most noble John Earl of Warwick, who was appointed Lieutenant of our said Lord the King to subdue, bind, and seize the said Robert Kett and the traitors aforesaid, did they at Dussindale, in the parishes of Thorpe and Sprowston, in the said county of Norfolk, on the 27th day of August, in the said third year of our said Lord the King that now is, in the said county of Norfolk, with banners unfurled, feloniously and traitorously murder and slay: And the same Robert Kett, and the other said traitors, on the said 27th day of August, by the favour of God, were, by the General, the most noble Earl of Warwick, and by other faithful subjects of the same our Lord the King then and there under the conduct of the same Earl of Warwick, honourably subdued and conquered: And thereupon the same Robert Kett, as a felonious traitor of our said Lord the King, did from the battle and place aforesaid, the same day and year, feloniously and traitorously betake himself as far as, and towards, Cawston,[3] in the said county of Norfolk, and was there taken and arrested by the lieges of our said Lord the King, for his wicked treasons aforesaid, against his due allegiance, and against the peace of our said Lord the King, his crown and dignity; and against the form of the Statute in this case lately made and provided.[4]

Sentence was passed accordingly. "It was determined that the aforesaid ... Robert Kett and William Kett be led by the aforesaid constable of the Tower as far as to the said Tower, and from thence be drawn through the midst of the city of London straight to the gallows at Tyburn, and on that gallows be hanged, and while yet alive, that they be cast on the ground, and the entrails of each one of them be taken out and burnt before them, while yet alive, and their heads be cut off, and their bodies divided into four parts; And that the heads and quarters of each of them be placed where our Lord the King shall appoint."[5]

The sentence was not carried out, for at some point shortly after the trial it was determined that the Ketts should be sent back to Norfolk to die. Justice must be seen to be done, and would be seen to best effect in those places where many of Kett's former followers had by now returned to their homes and occupations. Although the brothers were taken back to the Tower after the trial they were delivered on November 29 to the Sheriff of Norfolk, Sir Edmund Wyndham, who took them to Norwich. There on

December 1 Robert Kett was placed in fetters in the dungeons of the Guildhall. William may at first have shared the same confinement, but at some time before the day of execution he was removed to Wymondham, where he was to be hanged from the west tower of the Abbey. The executions took place on December 7. Robert Kett was drawn on a rough hurdle through the streets from the Guildhall to the Castle, from the walls of which he was hanged with his chains still on him. The body was left hanging until, many days later, it rotted, fell, and was removed.[6]

22. *The Ketts and the Rebellion*

Both Robert and William Kett were men of some substance. At the time of his death Robert's estate was valued at 1000 marks and his annual income computed to be £50. Both held considerable lands in the region of Wymondham, all of which were forfeit to the Crown after the rebellion. William was possessed of the old Westwode Chapel and of the manor of Choseley in Wymondham. Robert's lands are itemized in a document drawn up at the post mortem inquest held in Norwich Guildhall on January 13, 1550, before Henry Mynne, the Escheator of Norfolk. It was found that Kett held three properties: (1) the lands in Wymondham formerly belonging to the Hospital of Burton Lazars, which he had purchased from the Earl of Warwick and thereafter held *in capite* from the King, valued at £4 *per annum*, (2) lands known as Gunville's manor, held from the manor of Grishaugh in Wymondham for an annual rent of 4s. 8d. and valued at £13.6.8 *per annum*, part of which property was mortgaged to Robert Colyer, and (3) the tenements of Chillings and Tyes in Cakewick Field, near the marl-pits, held of the manor of Wymondham for an annual rent of 4½d. and valued at £1 *per annum*.[1] On May 18 all the lands of Robert Kett were granted by the Crown to Thomas Audley for his services in putting down the rebellion.

The Ketts had been men of property in Wymondham since at least the early thirteenth century. Robert's great uncle John is known to have held extensive lands in the area in the late fifteenth century, lands which probably passed to Robert's father, Thomas Kett, who also owned pasture land at Forncett. Thomas Kett's property must have been considerable, for the evidence suggests that four at least of his five sons each came to hold substantial portions. One son, John, is known to have died without heirs in 1530, when his properties passed to the eldest brother, William. Thomas, the youngest brother, was himself to be the progenitor of a highly prosperous line of Norfolk gentlemen.

What little is known of the Kett family derives largely from the researches of George Kett, at one time Mayor of Cambridge, who died in 1914.[2] The genealogy on pp. 146–7 summarizes part of his findings. The genealogy yields two surprises. It shows that the fortunes of the issue of Thomas Kett of Forncett suffered only partial and temporary reversal as a result of the events of 1549 and that Robert Kett may have been closely related by marriage to a number of his chief opponents, including Flowerdew and Warwick himself.

Robert's Kett's family do not seem to have been involved either in the rebellion or in the judicial reprisals which followed. Some of his sons, and possibly all of them, were still safely in their minority in 1549. The eldest, William, was restored to part of the family property some years afterwards – perhaps at the time he became of age. According to Russell, William was granted the lands at Westwode forfeited by his uncle, and these lands were sold many years later, in 1606, by one Richard Kett – probably the Richard, son of William, who appears in the genealogy as Robert Kett's eldest grandson.

Thomas Kett, the rebels' youngest brother, had died some sixteen years before the rising, and there is no suggestion that any of his four sons (who were probably older than the sons of Robert) were implicated in their uncles' unlawful activities. One of these, however, achieved notoriety in his own right: Francis Kett, Master of Arts, was burnt at Wymondham in 1588 for his heretical unitarian opinions. Another, Thomas junior, may have been the same Thomas Kett who in 1570 revealed to the authorities a conspiracy against the foreign settlers in Norwich.[3] From a third son, Adam, descends the line which was to emerge in prosperity in the nineteenth century (and which Russell mistakenly traces back to Robert Kett himself). Richard Kett, great-grandson of Adam, is known to have owned property in Roughton, near Cromer, in 1694. His son Henry parted with this but had obtained other lands at Dickleburgh and Seething before the mid eighteenth century. His son Thomas, who married (twice) into the family of the Gurneys, the bankers, enlarged the property at Seething, and when Russell wrote in 1859 this estate was enjoyed by Thomas Kett's son, George Samuel Kett, F.S.A.

Robert Kett's marriage to Alice Appleyard "is not directly proved, but practically proved by a series of extraordinary bits of circumstantial evidence."[4] If it is true that Kett married a daughter of Sir Nicholas Appleyard he was brother-in-law to Roger Appleyard and therefore uncle by marriage to the brothers John and Philip whom he captured early in the rising and who managed the guns against him during the first attack on Norwich. He would have been uncle also to their sister Frances, who was married to Sergeant Flowerdew's son William. And by Roger Appleyard's widow's second marriage Robert Kett was brought into affinity with the Robsarts and, had he lived a little longer, would have been connected by a chain of marriages to both

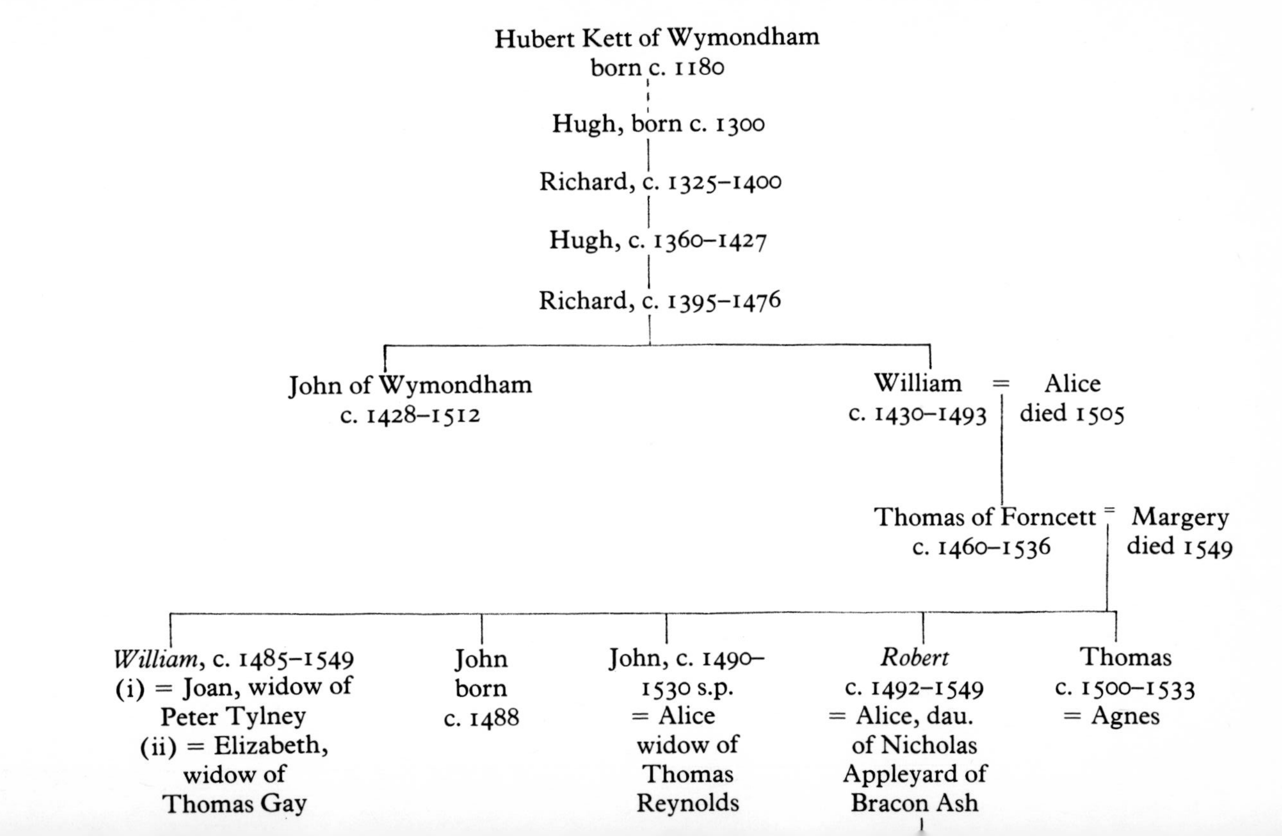

Hubert Kett of Wymondham
born c. 1180
Hugh, born c. 1300
Richard, c. 1325–1400
Hugh, c. 1360–1427
Richard, c. 1395–1476
John of Wymondham
c. 1428–1512
William
c. 1430–1493
=
Alice
died 1505
Thomas of Forncett
c. 1460–1536
=
Margery
died 1549
William, c. 1485–1549
(i) = Joan, widow of
Peter Tylney
(ii) = Elizabeth,
widow of
Thomas Gay
John
born
c. 1488
John, c. 1490–
1530 s.p.
= Alice
widow of
Thomas
Reynolds
Robert
c. 1492–1549
= Alice, dau.
of Nicholas
Appleyard of
Bracon Ash
Thomas
c. 1500–1533
= Agnes

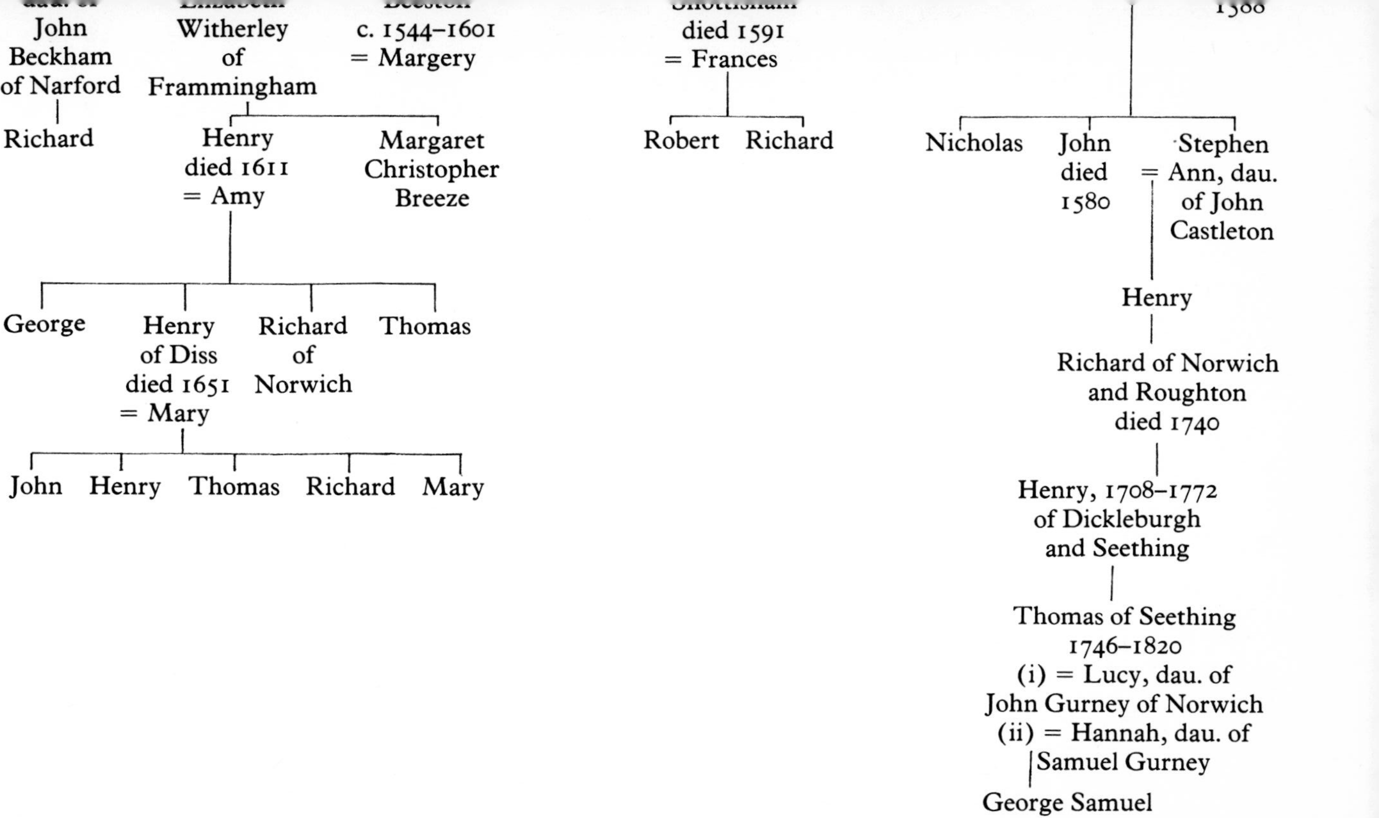
John
Beckham
of Narford
Richard
Witherley
of
Frammingham
c. 1544–1601
= Margery
Henry
died 1611
= Amy
Margaret
Christopher
Breeze
George
Henry
of Diss
died 1651
= Mary
Richard
of
Norwich
Thomas
John
Henry
Thomas
Richard
Mary
died 1591
= Frances
Robert
Richard
Nicholas
John
died
1580
Stephen
= Ann, dau.
of John
Castleton
Henry
Richard of Norwich
and Roughton
died 1740
Henry, 1708–1772
of Dickleburgh
and Seething
Thomas of Seething
1746–1820
(i) = Lucy, dau. of
John Gurney of Norwich
(ii) = Hannah, dau. of
Samuel Gurney
George Samuel

Warwick and Somerset. None of this need be unduly surprising, for the Norfolk gentry were for centuries bound together by complex networks of familial ties which were frequently crossed by political and ideological divisions. Kett's probable marriage does show, however, that far from being naturally opposed to Flowerdew and the Appleyards he was by birth and status of their kind.

Since Blomefield in the eighteenth century it has been customary to end the account of Kett's rebellion with passages from the records of the Norwich Court of Mayoralty for the years 1549 to 1554, which show the great sympathy for Kett and his cause which survived among the people after the collapse of the rising. For example:

On September 21, 1549, it was deposed that Robert Burnam, parish clerk of St. Gregory's, said, "There are too many gentlemen in England by five hundred."

On September 30, 1549, it was reported that Edmund Johnson, a labourer, had said in reply to an observation that Robert Kett would probably hang that "it should cost a thousand men's lives first."

On November 24, 1549, John Rooke was accused of saying, "Except the mercy of God, before Christmas, ye shall see as great a camp upon Mousehold as ever was, and if it be not then, it shall be of the spring of the year, and they shall come out of the Lord Protector's country to strengthen him." Somerset was by this time in the Tower, "which gave great offence to the commons, he being a good man."[5]

On February 12, 1550, George Redman deposed, "That John Redhad on Sunday at night, being the 10th of February, 1550, said, he would that Master Bakon [probably Henry Bacon, the Norwich alderman and merchant] and others, having on their gates the ragged staff, should take them down, for there were that are offended therewith, to the number of twenty persons and more: and he said, that the aforesaid ragged staff should be plucked down: and that afore it were Lammas day next coming, that Kett should be plucked down from the top of the castle; saying also that it was not meet to have any more Kings than one." The allusion is to Warwick, whose arms, the bear and ragged staff, had been displayed in Norwich after Dussindale.

On February 26, 1550, one said, "that five hundred of Mousehold men were gone to the Great Turk and the Dauphin, and will be here again by midsummer."[6]

That such things occurred need not surprise us when we remember that many of the inhabitants of Norwich had actively sympathized with Kett. What is a little surprizing is that, although perhaps nine or ten thousand of Kett's followers were still at large in Norfolk, the protest at his execution stopped short at the kind of ale-house bragging that most of these incidents suggest. Dussindale may have slain as many as three thousand of the rebels, and several hundreds more had died in streetfighting and on the gallows. But if the camp on Mousehold numbered only 12,000 (a conservative estimate), over 8,000 active rebels still returned unpunished to their homes. Why, after Warwick's withdrawal, did they take no further action? After the fall of Somerset the commons had more cause than ever to protest their position, but Dussindale had deprived them of leadership in Norfolk and dealt a severe blow to morale. The rebellion had collapsed, moreover, not only through the superior force of the opposition but also because of its failure, in six weeks of power, to do more than hold its ground. The survivors themselves must have seen that, even before the coming of Warwick and his cavalry, the rebellion had fallen into a stagnation which deprived it of any feasible purpose beyond mere day-to-day subsistence. What must have discouraged the Norfolk commons more than the lost battle, more than the corpses of the Ketts hanging for all to see, was the knowledge that rebellion, the extreme remedy, having been tried and having failed, their lot was irremediable.

The rebellion was largely conservative, its aim being to preserve the structure of the old manorial economy which, for more than a century, had been giving way to the modern system of individual proprietorship of which the outward symbol was the fence or enclosure. The rebellion was prompted not by any unusual represssion or extortion but, on the contrary, by unexpected marks of sympathy from the government. Kett demanded reforms which had already in outline received official approval and towards which Somerset, largely through enclosure commissions, was seen to be progressing. Had agrarian discontents not reached the pitch of open rebellion in 1548 and 1549 Somerset's programme might not have lost the Council's backing and might have been carried through to result in the enactment of many of the rebels' demands. The Northumberland government did in fact pass anti-enclosure laws a few years later, which shows that the promises held out by the Protector's commissions were by no means empty. Both Kett and Somerset, in their different ways, made the mistake of trying to accelerate agrarian reform to a pace which both excited the populace and frightened the aristocracy.

Somerset's injudicious use of enclosure commissions, his desire to be considered a generous and benevolent ruler, and the inevitable lenience with which the first risings were met, all encouraged the populace to think of him as "the good Duke" who would understand and support their complaints. (His reputation as the people's friend was further enhanced by his opponents' use of it against him at his trial.) Understand no doubt he did, but not for a moment did Somerset support or countenance rebellion. Recent scholarship[7] portrays Somerset not as an idealistic radical, the "good Duke" of popular tradition, but as an astute soldier and politician who adopted reasonable measures to meet the conditions of his time but who misjudged the effect of some of these measures – specifically his moves towards agrarian reform – on both the populace and the nobility in the summer of 1549. His cultivation of popularity, his lenience, and his open moves towards economic reform were all designed to promote general confidence and stability at home and to further his policies abroad, but ironically they ended by alienating the Council and stimulating many parts of the countryside to rebellion.

Of Kett himself we know very little – his name, his home, his occupation, his lands, and his whereabouts from early July 1549 to his death some five months later. He must have sympathized strongly with the discontented poor, their list of demands must represent a policy with which he was in general agreement, and his conduct of the early stages of the rising suggests his love of civil order. He was an effective leader and a competent administrator. He was certainly no ordinary rebel. He has been represented as a champion of the common man – the small farmer, the cottager, the artisan – which he was: but he was also the advocate of a modified feudal society from which all potentially disturbing economic and social forces would be rigorously excluded by imposition of legal controls. Kett appears to have led a rebellion not against but for a firmly fixed and hierarchical social structure.

The need for stability was widely felt in those days of rapid change. Not only was the face of the countryside changing with the erection of enclosures, and the structure of society altering with the new economy, but also the monasteries had disappeared, the forms of the old religion had been altered, and doctrine itself was being revised. All this was accompanied by an unprecedented rate of inflation and by the creation of new classes at the extremes of society: the very rich families already building the vast estates some of which were to last over three centuries, and the very poor, the droves of landless unemployed, the like of which England had not known before. Well might a man wonder where he stood! Kett stood for the stability of a social order based on a legally enforced network of mutual obligations, an order that had already almost passed away. The great feeling Kett aroused among the commons, which evidently survived his defeat and execution, was inextricably bound up with a longing for the security which the distant past was thought to have provided. An anonymous lament overheard in Norwich market place while Kett's body was still

hanging from the castle walls expresses this desire
harmony out of which the rebellion had grown.

> Oh Kett, God have mercy upon thy soul; and
> that the King's majesty and his Council shall be
> betwixt now and Midsummer eve, that of their
> thou shalt be taken down, by the grace of God, an
> not hanged up for winter store, and set a quietness
> and the ragged staff shall be taken down also of their own
> gentleness from the gentlemen's gates in this city, and to have
> no more kings' arms but one within this city under Christ but
> King Edward the sixth, God save his grace.[8]

Had either Somerset's agrarian programme or Kett's rebellion been effective, had the old laws been upheld and had what survived of the old economy been preserved, the course of English history would have been very different. The feudal system, modified as it had been over the centuries, instead of disappearing entirely in the early seventeenth century would have survived, as it did in Prussia, into the mid nineteenth century, and instead of being a leader in agriculture England would have been, like Prussia, extremely conservative. The basis of English economy would have been entirely different therefore, and the agricultural and industrial revolutions, instead of beginning in England, would have begun elsewhere – perhaps in the New World. The Civil Wars would perhaps not have occurred, for the small gentry who provided the backbone of the Parliamentary faction would have remained relatively powerless. Such speculations could be continued indefinitely but are of little value except to show that Kett stands at a turning point: his rebellion is one of the great might-have-beens of English history.

Bibliography

Adlard, George, *Amye Robsart and the Earl of Leicester* (London, 1870).

Anon. *Discourse of the Common Weal of the Realm of England,* ed. Elizabeth Lamond (Cambridge, 1893).

Beer, Barrett, L, "London and the Rebellions of 1548–1549", *Journal of British Studies,* 12 (1972).

Beer, Barrett L, *Northumberland: The Political Career of John Dudley, Earl of Warwick and Duke of Northumberland* (Kent, Ohio, 1973).

Bindoff, S. T, *Ket's Rebellion* (London, 1949).

Blomefield, Francis [and Charles Parkin], *An Essay towards a Topographical History of the County of Norfolk,* 2nd ed, 11 vols. (1805–1810).

Bradfer-Lawrence, H. L, *Castle Rising: A Short History and Description* (King's Lynn, 1954).

Brenan, Gerald, and Edward P. Statham, *The House of Howard,* 2 vols. (London, 1907).

Brook, V. J. K, *A Life of Archbishop Parker* (Oxford, 1962).

Bush, M. L, *The Government Policy of Protector Somerset* (London, 1975).

Clayton, Joseph, *Robert Kett and the Norfolk Rising* (London, 1912).

Dickens, A. G, "Some Popular Reactions to the Edwardian Reformation in Yorkshire", *Yorkshire Archaeological Journal,* 34 (1939).

Drummond, Humphry, *Our Men in Scotland: Sir Ralph Sadler, 1507–1587* (London, 1969).

Edward VI, *The Chronicle and Political Papers of King Edward VI,* ed. W. K. Jordan (Ithaca, New York, 1966).

Fletcher, Anthony, *Tudor Rebellions* (London, 1968).

Foss, Michael, *Tudor Portraits: Success and Failure of an Age* (London, 1973).

Frere, H. T. Bartle, *Amy Robsart of Wymondham* (London, 1937).

Green Barbara, *Norwich Castle: A Fortress for Nine Centuries* (Norwich, 1970).

Groves, R, *Rebel's Oak: The Story of the Great Rebellion of 1549* (London, 1947).

Hayward, Sir John, *Life and Reign of King Edward the Sixth* (1610).

Holinshed, Rafael, *Chronicles of England, Scotland, and Ireland* (1578).

Hooker, John, *The Description of the Citie of Excester* (1575).

Hooker, John, "The Discourse and Discovery of the Life of Sir Peter Carewe" in *Calendar of the Carew Manuscripts ... at Lambeth,* ed. J. S. Brewer and William Bullen (London. 1867).

Hughes, Paul, and James F. Larkin (eds.), *Tudor Royal Proclamations,* 3 vols. (New Haven, Connecticut, 1964).

Jordan, W. K, *Edward VI, The Young King: The Protectorship of the Duke of Somerset* (Cambridge, Massachusetts, 1968).

Kerridge, Eric, *Agrarian Problems in the Sixteenth Century and After* (London, 1969).
Kett, L. M, *The Ketts of Norfolk: A Yeoman Family* (London, 1921).
Ketton-Cremer, R. W, *Felbrigg: The Story of a House* (London, 1962).
Ketton-Cremer, R. W, *Norfolk in the Civil War* (London, 1970).
LeStrange, Richard, *Monasteries of Norfolk* (King's Lynn, 1973).
Mander, R. P, "Wymondham Abbey and the Robert Kett Rebellion of 1549", *East Anglian Magazine*, 6 (1947).
Neville, Alexander, *De furoribus Norfolciensium Ketto duce* (1575).
Outhwaite, R. B, *Inflation in Tudor and Early Stuart England* (London, 1969).
Pevsner, Nikolaus, *The Buildings of England: North West and South Norfolk* (London, 1962).
Pollard, A. F, *England under Protector Somerset* (London, 1900).
Pollard, A. F, *History of England from the Accession of Edward VI to the Death of Elizabeth* (London, 1913).
Ravensdale, J. R, "Landbeach in 1549: Kett's Rebellion in Miniature" in *East Anglian Studies*, ed. Lionel M. Munby (Cambridge, 1968).
Rose-Troup, Frances, *The Western Rebellion of 1549* (London, 1913).
Rowse, A. L, *Tudor Cornwall* (London, 1951).
Russell, Frederick W, *Kett's Rebellion in Norfolk* (London, 1859).
Simpson, Alan, *The Wealth of the Gentry 1540–1660* (Cambridge, 1961).
Sotherton, Nicholas, *The Commoyson in Norfolk 1549*, B. M. Harl. MS. 1576, fol. 564ff.
Strype, John, *Life of Parker* (1711).
Tawney, R. H, *The Agrarian Problem in the Sixteenth Century* (London, 1912).
Tawney, R. H, and Eileen Power, *Tudor Economic Documents*, 3 vols. (London, 1924).
Thomas, J. G. Tansley, "A Brief History of Wymondham Abbey" in *The Abbey Church of St. Mary and St. Thomas of Canterbury in Wymondham* (Wymondham, 1957).
Tytler, P. F, *England under the Reigns of Edward VI and Mary*, 2 vols. (London, 1839).
Vyse, J. W. M, "The Evidences of Kett's Rebellion", *Norfolk Archaeology*, 26 (1938).
Woodman, A. Vere, "The Buckinghamshire and Oxfordshire Rising", *Oxoniensia*, 22 (1957).
Wyndham, H. A, *A Family History 1410–1688: The Wyndhams of Norfolk and Somerset* (London, 1939).

Footnotes

Chapter 2

[1] For a recent reappraisal of these matters see Eric Kerridge, *Agrarian Problems in the Sixteenth Century and After* (London, 1969), especially pp. 17–93.

[2] The figures are from Alan Simpson, *The Wealth of the Gentry 1540–1660* (Cambridge, 1961), pp. 182–184.

[3] By the 1550s agricultural prices exceeded those of the 1530s by ninety-five per cent (R. B. Outhwaite, *Inflation in Tudor and Early Stuart England* (London, 1969), pp. 13 and 43.)

[4] See the edition of this text by Elizabeth Lamond (Cambridge, 1893).

[5] M. L. Bush, *The Government Policy of Protector Somerset* (London, 1975), pp. 1, 41, and 62–63.

Chapter 3

[1]Tudor Royal Proclamations, ed. Paul L. Hughes and James F. Larkin (New Haven, Connecticut, 1964), I, 425–427.

[2] Hughes and Larkin, I, 427–429. The Acts referred to are 4 Hen VII, c. 19; 6 Hen VIII, c. 5; 7 Hen VIII, c. 1; 25 Hen VIII, c. 13; and 27 Hen VIII, c. 1.

[3] Bush, pp. 74–83.

[4] Bush, p. 78.

[5] Bush, pp. 52–53.

[6] Bush, p. 55.

[7] Hughes and Larkin, I, 453.

[8] Hughes and Larkin, I, 461.

[9] Hughes and Larkin, I, 463.

[10] Bush, pp. 73–83.

[11] Hughes and Larkin, I, 474.

[12] Hughes and Larkin, I, 475–476.

[13] Bush, pp. 87–88 and *passim.*

Chapter 4

[1] Most of the following details of the history of the Priory are drawn from J. G. Tansley Thomas, "A Brief History of Wymondham Abbey" in *The Abbey Church of St. Mary and St. Thomas of Canterbury in Wymondham* (Wymondham, 1957). See also R. P. Mander, "Wymondham Abbey and the Robert Kett Rebellion of 1549", *East Anglian Magazine*, 6 (1947), 605–610.

[2] L. M. Kett, *The Ketts of Norfolk: A Yeoman Family* (London, 1921), p. 56.

[3] For details on the family see chapter 22 below.

[4] Kett, p. 57. (Ferrers soon left Wymondham to become, in 1539, Archdeacon of Suffolk. He died in 1548 and is buried in Wymondham church where his impressive monument can still be seen.)

[5] H. L. Bradfer-Lawrence, *Castle Rising: A Short History and Description* (King's Lynn, 1954).

Chapter 5

[1] Barrett L. Beer, "London and the Rebellions of 1548–1549" in *Journal of British Studies*, 12 (1972), pp. 15–38.

[2] A .G . Dickens, "Some Popular Reactions to the Edwardian Reformation in Yorkshire," *Yorkshire Archaeological Journal*, 34 (1939), pp. 158ff.

[3] A. Vere Woodman, "The Buckinghamshire and Oxfordshire Rising," *Oxoniensia*, 22 (1957), pp. 78ff.

[4] The most important sources are John Hooker, *The Description of the Citie of Excester* (1575) and "The Discourse and Discovery of the Life of Sir Peter Carewe" in *Calendar of the Carew Manuscripts . . . at Lambeth*, ed. J. S. Brewer and W. Bullen (London, 1867); Frances Rose-Troup, *The Western Rebellion of 1549* (London, 1913); and A. L. Rowse, *Tudor Cornwall* (London, 1951). There is a useful summary in Anthony Fletcher, *Tudor Rebellions* (London, 1968).

Chapter 6

[1] This was the government's estimate at the time, cited, for example, in the indictment drawn up for Kett's trial.

Chapter 7

[1] The fortunes of the Howards are chronicled in Gerald Brenan and Edward P. Statham, *The House of Howard*, 2 vols. (London, 1907).

[2] Both Anne Boleyn and Catherine Howard were nieces of the third Duke of Norfolk.

[3] Father of Sir Thomas.

[4] This situation among the Norfolk gentry evidently persisted into the Civil War: see R. W. Ketton-Cremer, *Norfolk in the Civil War* (1970).

Chapter 8

[1] These details are drawn from Kett (1921).

[2] Humphry Drummond, *Our Man in Scotland: Sir Ralph Sadlier, 1507–1587* (London, 1969), p. 162.

[3] The two names *Wymondham* and *Wyndham* are both pronounced WIND'AM: it is thought that the family name, now often spelt *Windham*, derives from the name of the town. The history of the family is well chronicled: see H. A. Wyndham, *A Family History 1410–1688: The Wyndhams of Norfolk and Somerset* (London, 1939), and R. W. Ketton-Cremer, *Felbrigg: The Story of House* (London, 1962).

[4] He was granted lands from the Priory of Beeston Regis near Sheringham.

[5] Brenan and Statham, II, 381.

[6] Francis Blomefield and Charles Parkin, *Topographical History of . . .*

Norfolk, 2nd. ed. (London, 1805–1810), III, 225.

[7] The Gawdy genealogies are uncertain because John or Thomas Gawdy of Harleston had, by three successive wives, three sons each christened Thomas and each to become an eminent lawyer. The father is sometimes confused with the eldest son, who was probably Kett's prisoner.

[8] See chapter 19 below.

Chapter 9

[1] Quoted from Blomefield, III, 228–229.

[2] See Barbara Green, *Norwich Castle: A Fortress for Nine Centuries* (Norwich, 1970).

[3] Blomefield, III, 226.

Chapter 10

[1] F. W. Russell, *Kett's Rebellion in Norfolk* (London, 1859), pp. 203–204. The original is in B. M. Harl. MS. 304, f. 75.

[2] Blomefield, III, 226.

[3] Russell, p. 47.

[4] B. M. Harl. MS., 1576, fol. 564.

Chapter 11

[1] B. M. Harl, MS., 304, fol. 75. (Russell, pp. 48–56.)

[2] Blomefield, III, 212.

[3] Anthony Fletcher, *Tudor Rebellions* (London, 1968). p. 72. Blomefield, III, 193

[4] S. T. Bindoff, *Ket's Rebellion* (London, 1949), p. 9.

[5] Bindoff, p. 13.

[6] Fletcher, p. 74.

Chapter 12

[1] The standard biography of Parker is John Strype's *Life of Parker* (1711). This is now supplemented by V. J. K. Brook, *A Life of Archbishop Parker* (Oxford, 1962).

[2] J. R. Ravensdale, "Landbeach in 1549: Ket's Rebellion in Miniature" in *East Anglian Studies*, ed. Lionel M. Munby (Cambridge, 1968), p. 155.

Chapter 15

[1] A small modern plaque now indicates the approximate place of Sheffield's death. It replaces the old slab (reproduced by Russell) bearing the letter "S", which has disappeared and may still lie beneath the modern pavement.

Chapter 16

[1] Russell, p. 107.

Chapter 17

[1] A. F. Pollard, *England Under Protector Somerset* (London, 1900), p. 241.

[2] P. F. Tytler, *England Under the Reigns of Edward VI and Mary* (London, 1839), I, 193.

[3] Here and elsewhere my interpretation of Warwick's motives is indebted to Barrett L. Beer, *Northumberland: The Political Career of John Dudley, Earl of Warwick and Duke of Northumberland* (Kent, Ohio, 1973).
[4] Hughes and Larkin, I, 481.
[5] Beer, *Northumberland*, pp. 76–77 and 87.
[6] Bush, pp. 74–75.
[7] Blomefield, III, 254.

Chapter 18
[1] "alias Poignard, a man of great valour" (Blomefield, III, 248).
[2] Blomefield, III, 252.

Chapter 19
[1] Russell, pp. 151–153.
[2] For the story of Amy Robsart, her family and her marriage, see George Adlard, *Amye Robsart and the Earl of Leicester* (London, 1870), and H. T. Bartle Frere, *Amy Robsart of Wymondham* (London, 1937).

Chapter 20
[1] Calendar of State Papers, Domestic, Edw VI, viii, 4.
[2] Calendar of State Papers, Spanish, ix, 448.
[3] Hughes and Larkin, I, 483.
[4] Hughes and Larkin, I, 483.

Chapter 21
[1] Russell, pp. 215–217. The original is in Latin.
[2] Russell, pp. 224–226. The original is in Latin.
[3] About four miles north of Swannington where Kett was actually captured.
[4] Russell, pp. 220–223. The original is in Latin.
[5] Russell, p. 227. The original is in Latin.
[6] A large inscription in stone affixed to the external wall of the castle keep now commemorates the event. It was erected in 1949 "by the citizens of Norwich in reparation and honour to a notable and courageous leader in the long struggle of the common people of England to escape from a servile life into the freedom of just conditions".

Chapter 22
[1] The document is reprinted in Russell, pp. 228–235.
[2] Published by L. M. Kett under the title *The Ketts of Norfolk* in 1921. The genealogy given by Russell is shown to be seriously in error.
[3] Blomefield, III, 284.
[4] Kett, pp. 56–57.
[5] Blomefield, III, 257.
[6] Blomefield, III, 257–258. Cf. Russell, pp. 162–164. Cf. also *Tudor Economic Documents*, ed. R. H. Tawney and Eileen Power (London, 1924), I, 47–53.
See especially Bush (1975).
[8] Blomefield, III, 258.

Index

HONI SOIT QVY MAL Y PENSE
NORDOVICV
¶The Defcription of the Citie of Norwich, with